Intro Chem Course Noteboook

Welcome to Intro Chem.

This is your personal course notebook for assisting you with learning the Intro Chem course material while you are viewing the online modules for each Unit.

Please refer to your course information sheets and the course website on Avenue to Learn for additional information about the course.

This notebook belongs to:______________________________________

McMaster University

Arthur Bourns Building, ABB 156

1280 Main Street West

Hamilton, ON, L8S 4M1

Resources Available to Help With This Course:

- Web modules in Avenue to Learn
- Course Notebook
- Course Textbook (Petrucci, 10th edition)
- Help Centre in ABB 307
- Instructor and Lab Coordinator Office Hours
- Tutorials
- Lists of Learning Objectives
- In-class Slides
- Recommended Practice Questions
- Avenue to Learn Discussion Forum
- Private Tutor (see list in Avenue to Learn)

Add in other resources if you have them:

-
-
-

Intro Chem Unit Topics

- Unit 1 – Introduction
- Unit 2 – Fundamental Skills Review
- Unit 3 – Atomic Theory and Structure
- Unit 4 – Periodic Trends
- Unit 5 – Chemical Bonding
- Unit 6 – Solubility and Chemical Equilibrium
- Unit 7 – Acid-Base Chemistry
- Unit 8 – Thermochemistry
- Unit 9 – Entropy and Free Energy
- Unit 10 – Energy and Electrochemistry

CHEMISTRY
1A03

UNIT 1 - Introduction

How to Navigate the Modules

MODULE 1

Introduction I

WHAT IS CHEMISTRY?
?

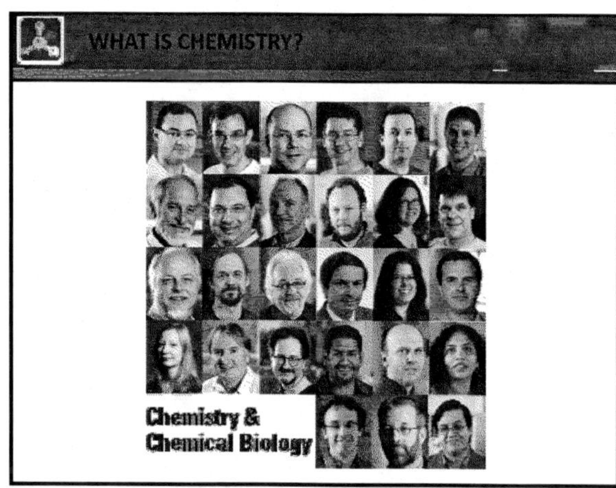
WHAT IS CHEMISTRY?
Chemistry &
Chemical Biology

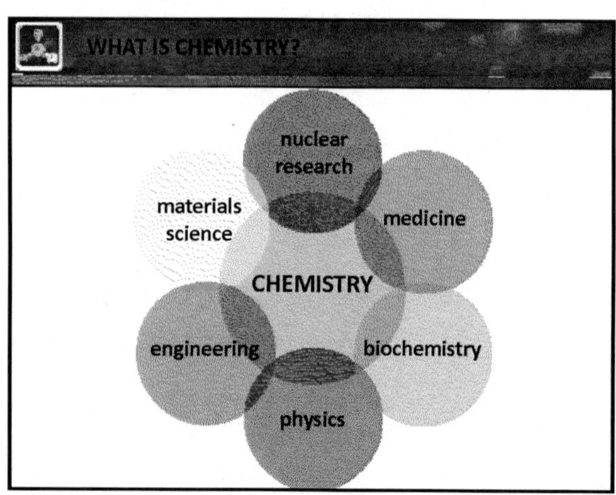
WHAT IS CHEMISTRY?
nuclear
research
materials
science
medicine
CHEMISTRY
engineering
biochemistry
physics

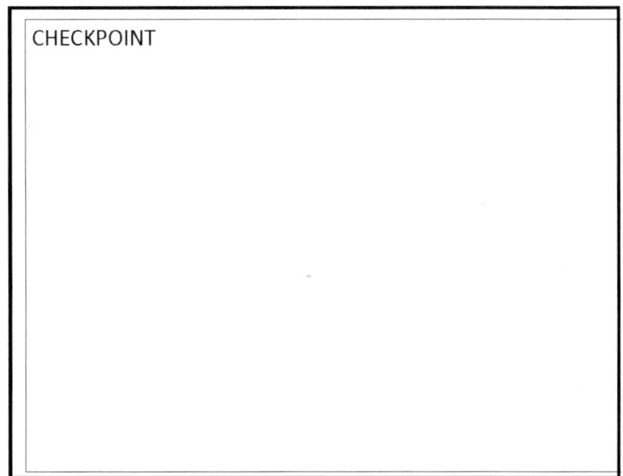
CHECKPOINT

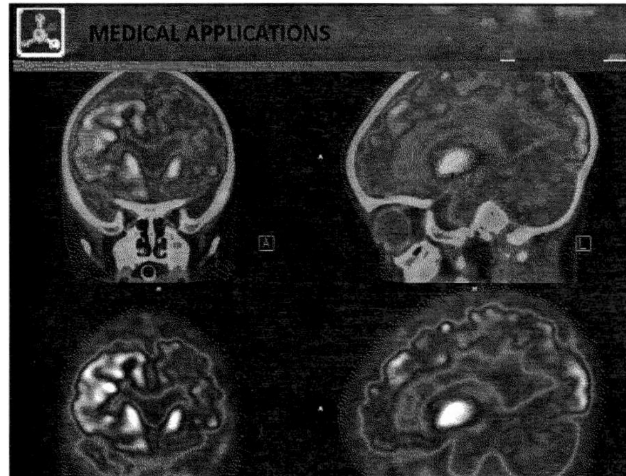
MEDICAL APPLICATIONS

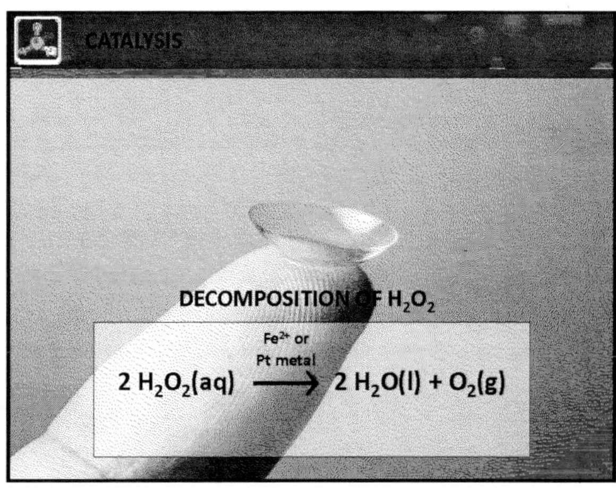
CATALYSIS
DECOMPOSITION OF H_2O_2
Fe^{2+} or Pt metal
$2\,H_2O_2(aq) \longrightarrow 2\,H_2O(l) + O_2(g)$

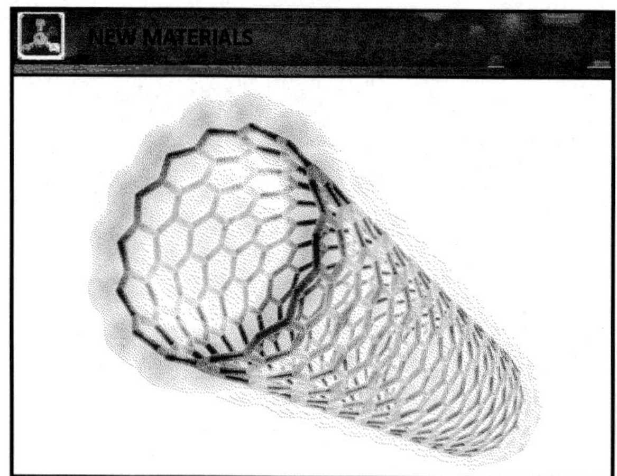
NEW MATERIALS

CLEANER FUELS
$2\ H_2(g) + O_2(g) \rightarrow 2\ H_2O(l)$

RECREATIONAL CHEMISTRY

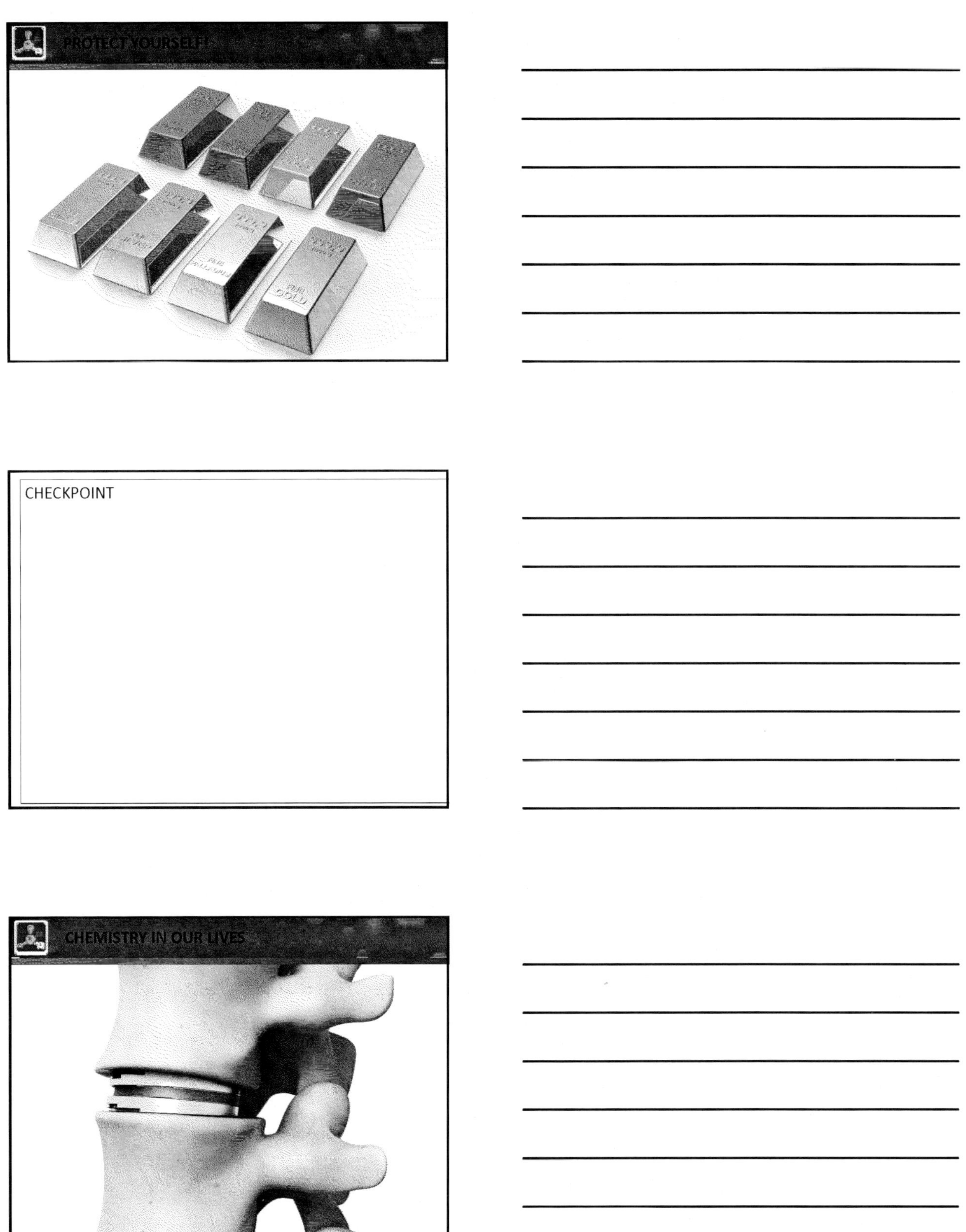
PROTECT YOURSELF!
CHECKPOINT
CHEMISTRY IN OUR LIVES

CHEMISTRY IN OUR LIVES

Radiochemist
Pharmacist
Drug developer
Petroleum
Geochemist
Doctor
Spectroscopist
Energy
Forensic scientist
Pharmaceuticals
Agrochemicals
Research and development

Unit 1

Most important concepts:

-
-
-
-
-
-
-
-
-
-
-
-

Unit 1

Questions I have:

-
-
-
-
-
-
-
-
-
-
-
-

UNIT 2
Fundamental Skills Review

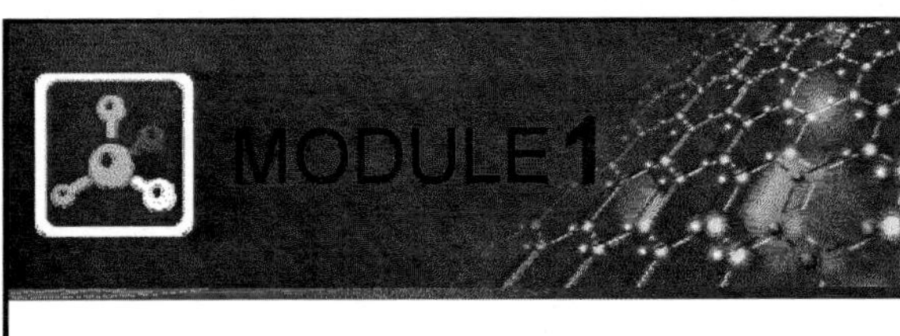

Fundamental Skills Review I

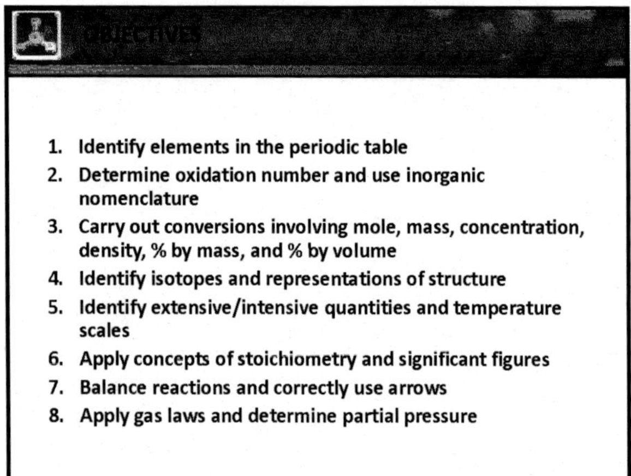
OBJECTIVES
1. Identify elements in the periodic table
2. Determine oxidation number and use inorganic nomenclature
3. Carry out conversions involving mole, mass, concentration, density, % by mass, and % by volume
4. Identify isotopes and representations of structure
5. Identify extensive/intensive quantities and temperature scales
6. Apply concepts of stoichiometry and significant figures
7. Balance reactions and correctly use arrows
8. Apply gas laws and determine partial pressure

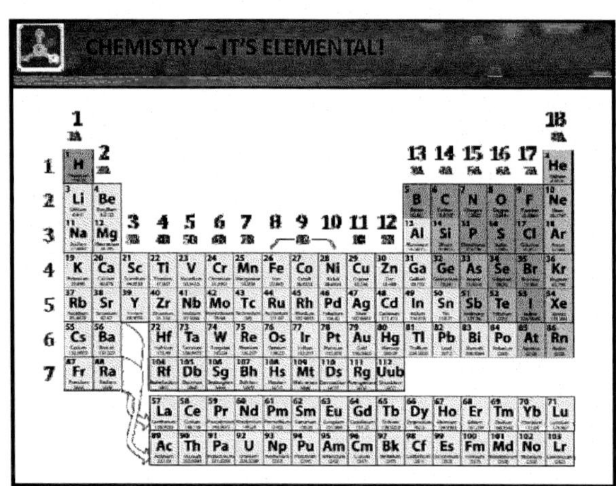
CHEMISTRY – IT'S ELEMENTAL!

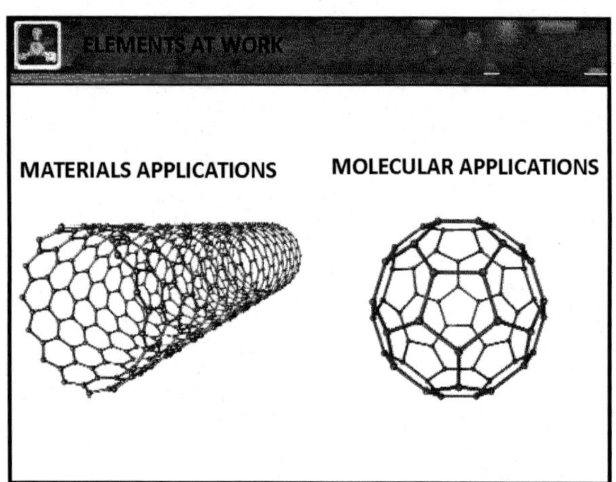
ELEMENTS AT WORK
MATERIALS APPLICATIONS
MOLECULAR APPLICATIONS

ELEMENTS AT WORK AND PLAY

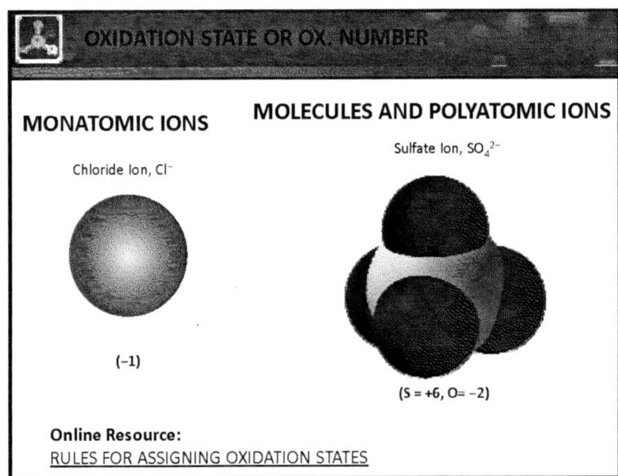
OXIDATION STATE OR OX. NUMBER
MONATOMIC IONS
MOLECULES AND POLYATOMIC IONS
Chloride Ion, Cl^-
Sulfate Ion, SO_4^{2-}
(-1)
(S = +6, O= -2)
Online Resource:
RULES FOR ASSIGNING OXIDATION STATES

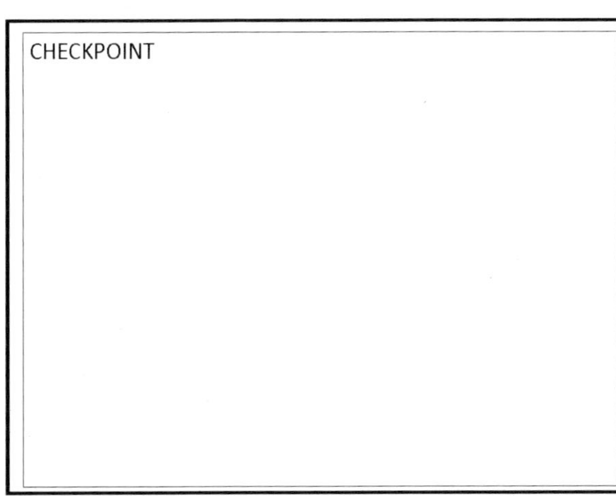
CHECKPOINT

NOMENCLATURE

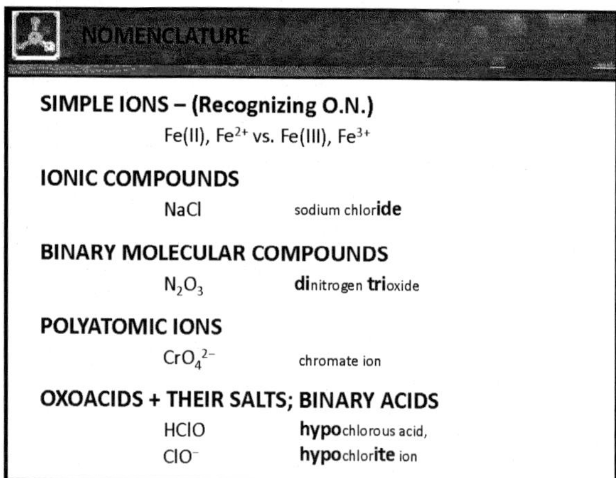
NOMENCLATURE
SIMPLE IONS – (Recognizing O.N.)
Fe(II), Fe^{2+} vs. Fe(III), Fe^{3+}
IONIC COMPOUNDS
NaCl sodium chloride
BINARY MOLECULAR COMPOUNDS
N_2O_3 dinitrogen trioxide
POLYATOMIC IONS
CrO_4^{2-} chromate ion
OXOACIDS + THEIR SALTS; BINARY ACIDS
HClO hypochlorous acid,
ClO^- hypochlorite ion

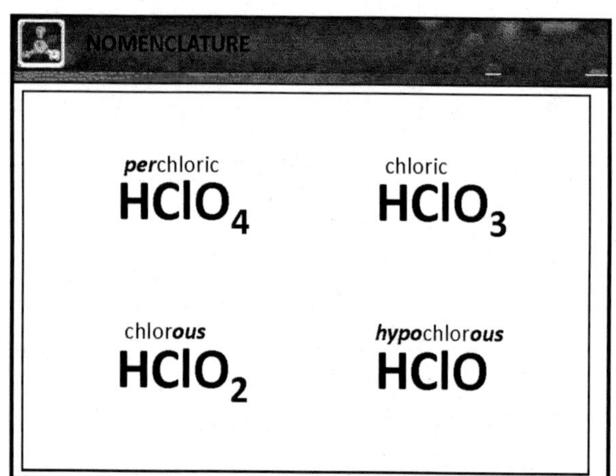
NOMENCLATURE
perchloric
$HClO_4$
chloric
$HClO_3$
chlorous
$HClO_2$
hypochlorous
HClO

MOLE

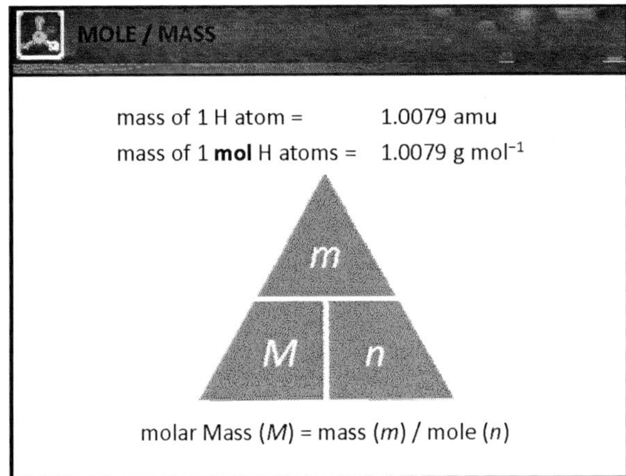
MOLE / MASS
mass of 1 H atom = 1.0079 amu
mass of 1 **mol** H atoms = 1.0079 g mol^{-1}
m
M
n
molar Mass (M) = mass (m) / mole (n)

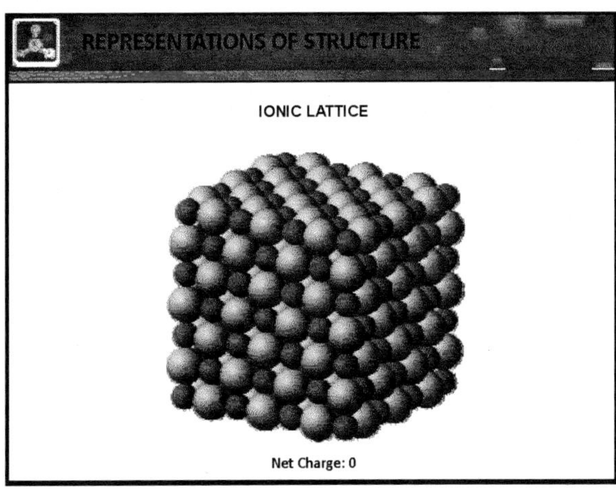
REPRESENTATIONS OF STRUCTURE
IONIC LATTICE
Net Charge: 0

REPRESENTATIONS OF STRUCTURE

EMPIRICAL FORMULA

CH_2O Simplest Atom-Ratio

MOLECULAR FORMULA

$C_2H_4O_2$ Actual Atom-Ratio

STRUCTURAL FORMULA

H–C(H)(H)–C(=O)–O–H Connectivity

REPRESENTATIONS OF STRUCTURE

REPRESENTATION:	EXAMPLE:
CONDENSED STRUCTURAL FORMULA	CH_3COOH
LINE-ANGLE STICK FORMULA	O, OH
BALL & STICK MODEL	
SPACE FILLING MODEL	

CHECKPOINT

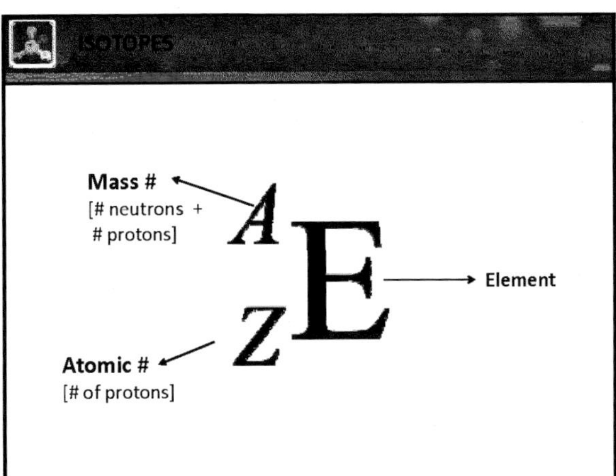
ISOTOPES
Mass #
[# neutrons +
protons]
A
E
Element
Z
Atomic #
[# of protons]

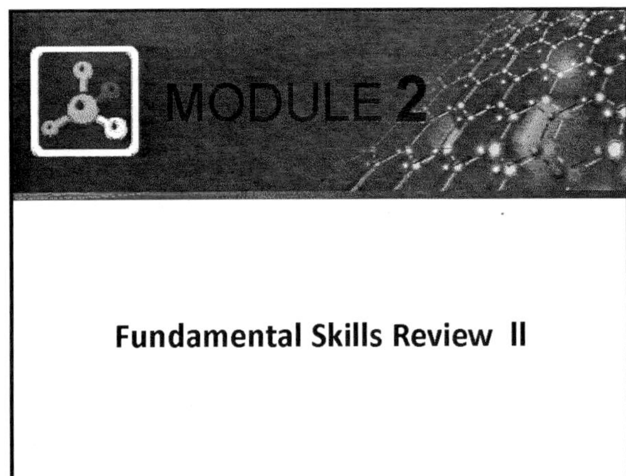
MODULE 2
Fundamental Skills Review II

EXTENSIVE AND INTENSIVE PROPERTIES
1 MOL OF H2O
1 MOL OF H2O

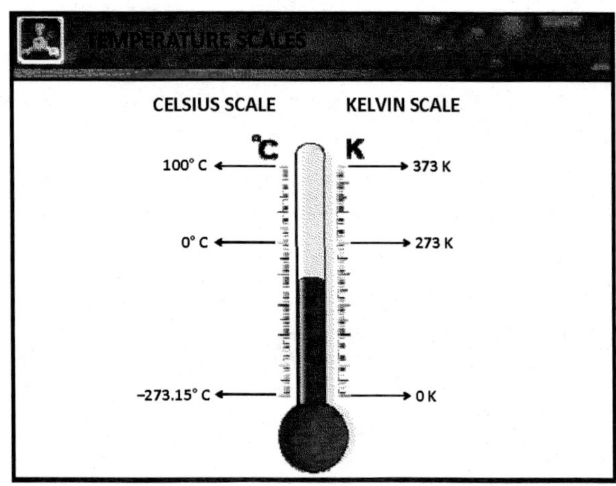

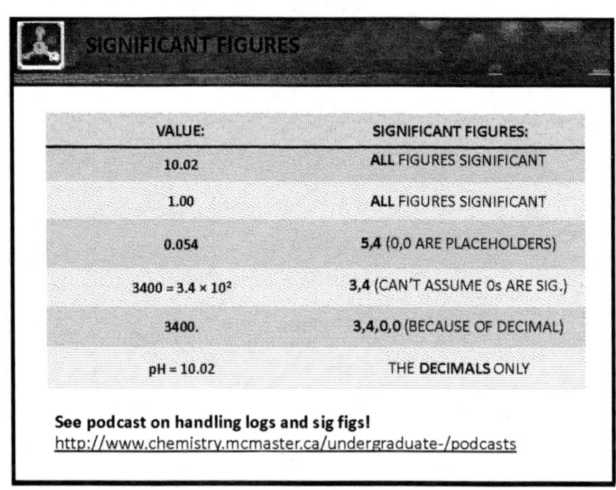

VALUE:	SIGNIFICANT FIGURES:
10.02	**ALL** FIGURES SIGNIFICANT
1.00	**ALL** FIGURES SIGNIFICANT
0.054	**5,4** (0,0 ARE PLACEHOLDERS)
$3400 = 3.4 \times 10^2$	**3,4** (CAN'T ASSUME 0s ARE SIG.)
3400.	**3,4,0,0** (BECAUSE OF DECIMAL)
pH = 10.02	THE **DECIMALS** ONLY

See podcast on handling logs and sig figs!
http://www.chemistry.mcmaster.ca/undergraduate-/podcasts

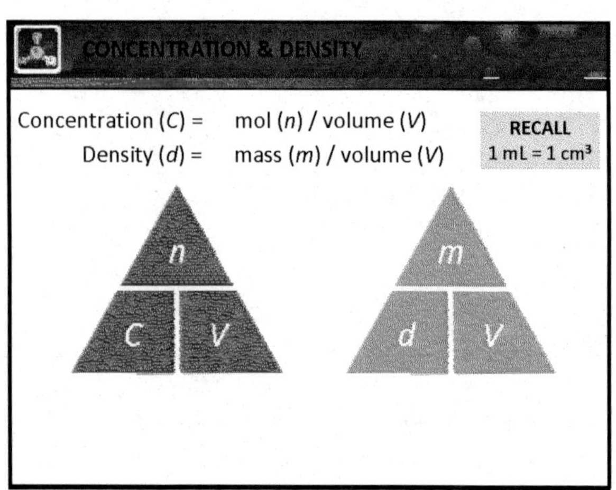

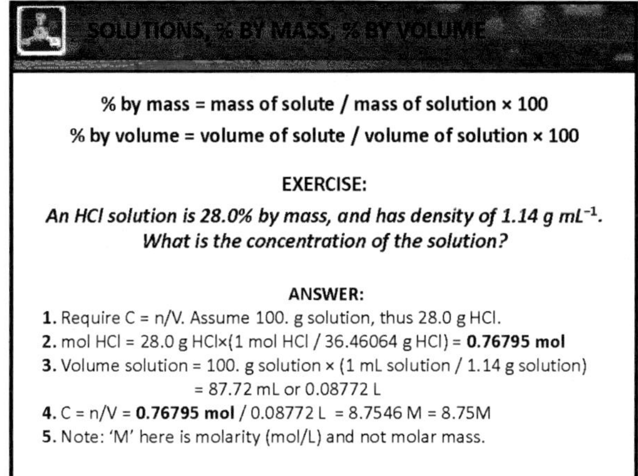

SOLUTIONS, % BY MASS, % BY VOLUME
% by mass = mass of solute / mass of solution × 100
% by volume = volume of solute / volume of solution × 100
EXERCISE:
An HCl solution is 28.0% by mass, and has density of 1.14 g mL^{-1}. What is the concentration of the solution?
ANSWER:
1. Require C = n/V. Assume 100. g solution, thus 28.0 g HCl.
2. mol HCl = 28.0 g HCl×(1 mol HCl / 36.46064 g HCl) = 0.76795 mol
3. Volume solution = 100. g solution × (1 mL solution / 1.14 g solution) = 87.72 mL or 0.08772 L
4. C = n/V = 0.76795 mol / 0.08772 L = 8.7546 M = 8.75M
5. Note: 'M' here is molarity (mol/L) and not molar mass.

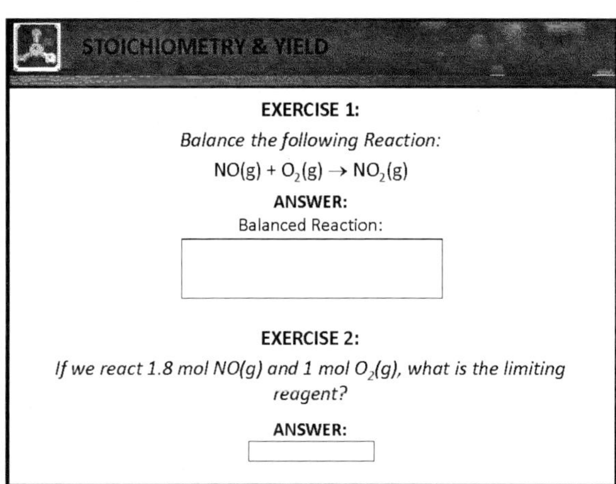

STOICHIOMETRY & YIELD
EXERCISE 1:
Balance the following Reaction:
$NO(g) + O_2(g) \rightarrow NO_2(g)$
ANSWER:
Balanced Reaction:
EXERCISE 2:
If we react 1.8 mol NO(g) and 1 mol O_2(g), what is the limiting reagent?
ANSWER:

STOICHIOMETRY & YIELD

EXERCISE 3:

$2\ NO(g) + O_2(g) \rightarrow 2\ NO_2(g)$

From 1.8 mol NO(g) and 1 mol O_2(g) what is the theoretical yield (mol) of NO_2(g)?

ANSWER:

1.8 mol, since NO is limiting reagent,

EXERCISE 4:

If we actually get 1.6 mol NO_2(g), what is the percent yield?

ANSWER:

$$\text{percent yield} = \frac{\text{actual yield}}{\text{theoretical yield}} \times 100\% =$$

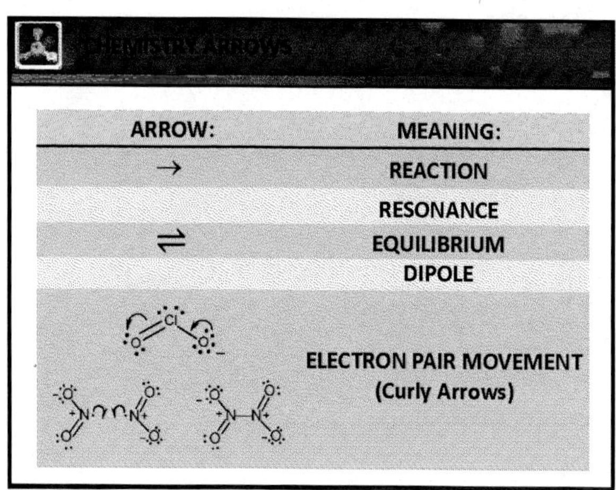

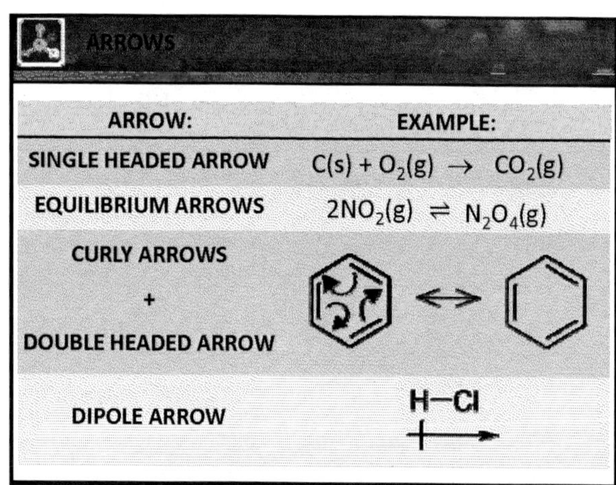

GAS LAWS

$$PV = nRT$$

BOYLE	CHARLES	AVOGADRO
$V \propto \frac{1}{P}$	$V \propto T$	$V \propto n$

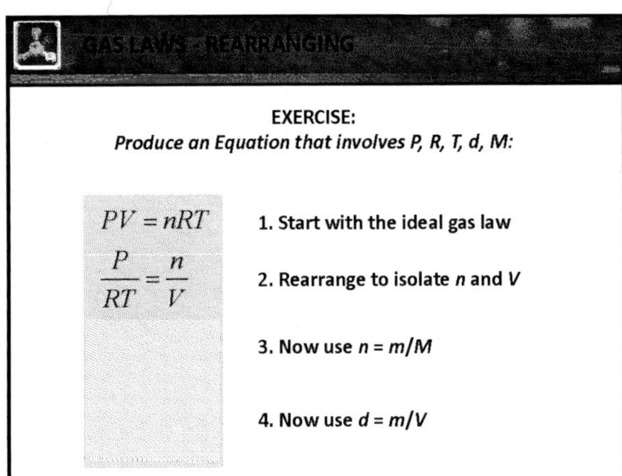
GAS LAWS - REARRANGING
EXERCISE:
Produce an Equation that involves P, R, T, d, M:
$PV = nRT$
$\frac{P}{RT} = \frac{n}{V}$
1. Start with the ideal gas law
2. Rearrange to isolate n and V
3. Now use n = m/M
4. Now use d = m/V

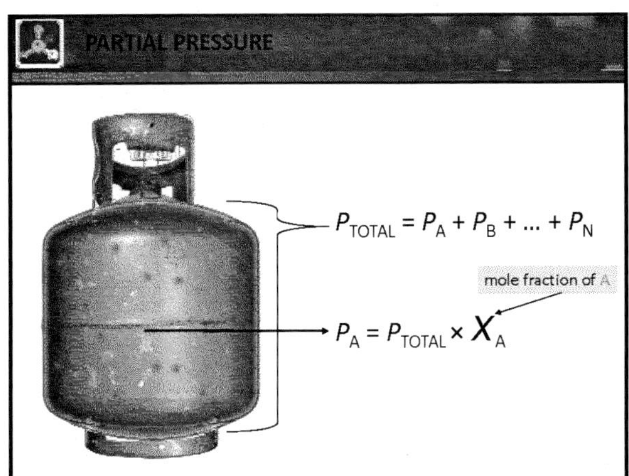
PARTIAL PRESSURE
$P_{TOTAL} = P_A + P_B + \ldots + P_N$
mole fraction of A
$P_A = P_{TOTAL} \times X_A$

CHECKPOINT

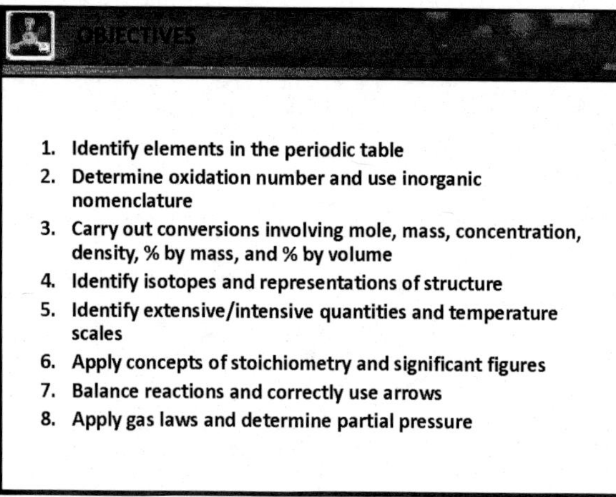
OBJECTIVES
1. Identify elements in the periodic table
2. Determine oxidation number and use inorganic nomenclature
3. Carry out conversions involving mole, mass, concentration, density, % by mass, and % by volume
4. Identify isotopes and representations of structure
5. Identify extensive/intensive quantities and temperature scales
6. Apply concepts of stoichiometry and significant figures
7. Balance reactions and correctly use arrows
8. Apply gas laws and determine partial pressure

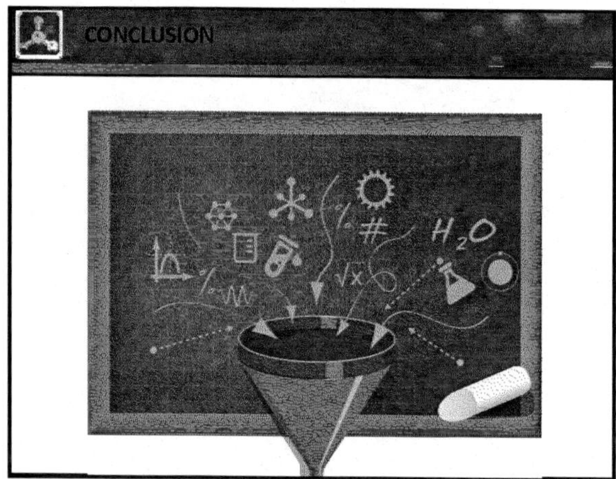
CONCLUSION
H2O

Unit 2

Most important concepts:

-
-
-
-
-
-
-
-
-
-
-
-

Unit 2

Questions I have:

-
-
-
-
-
-
-
-
-
-
-
-

UNIT 3 - Atomic Structure and Theory

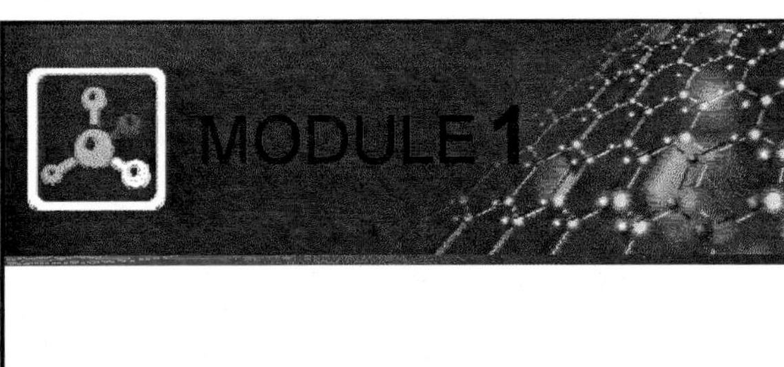

Atomic Structure and Theory I

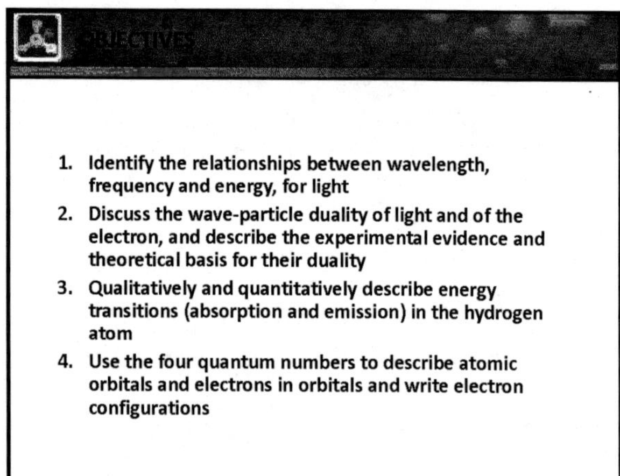

OBJECTIVES
1. Identify the relationships between wavelength, frequency and energy, for light
2. Discuss the wave-particle duality of light and of the electron, and describe the experimental evidence and theoretical basis for their duality
3. Qualitatively and quantitatively describe energy transitions (absorption and emission) in the hydrogen atom
4. Use the four quantum numbers to describe atomic orbitals and electrons in orbitals and write electron configurations

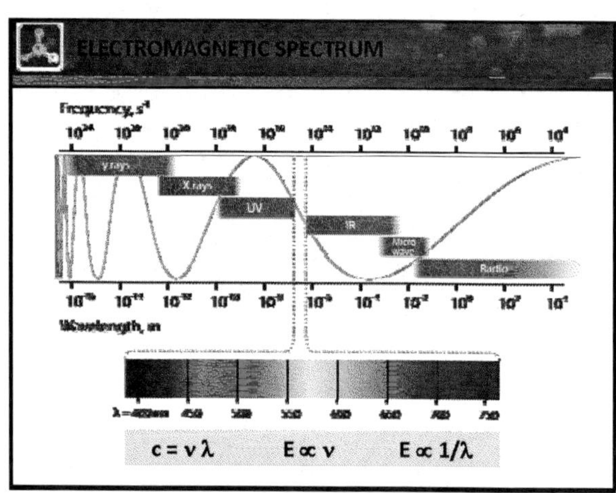

ELECTROMAGNETIC SPECTRUM
Frequency, s⁻¹
X rays
UV
IR
Radio
Wavelength, m
c = v λ
E ∝ v
E ∝ 1/λ

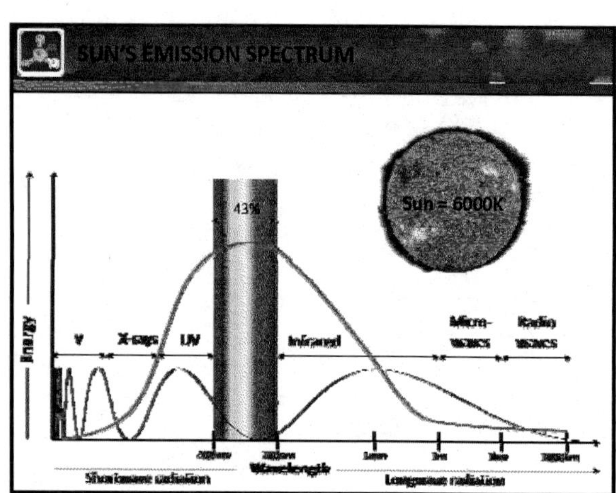

SUN'S EMISSION SPECTRUM
43%
Sun = 6000K
Energy
X-rays
UV
Infrared
Micro-waves
Radio waves
Wavelength

ATOMIC SPECTRA

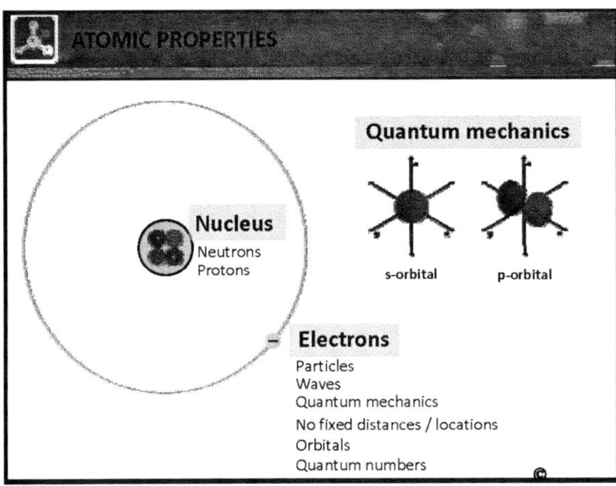
ATOMIC PROPERTIES
Quantum mechanics
s-orbital
p-orbital
Nucleus
Neutrons
Protons
Electrons
Particles
Waves
Quantum mechanics
No fixed distances / locations
Orbitals
Quantum numbers

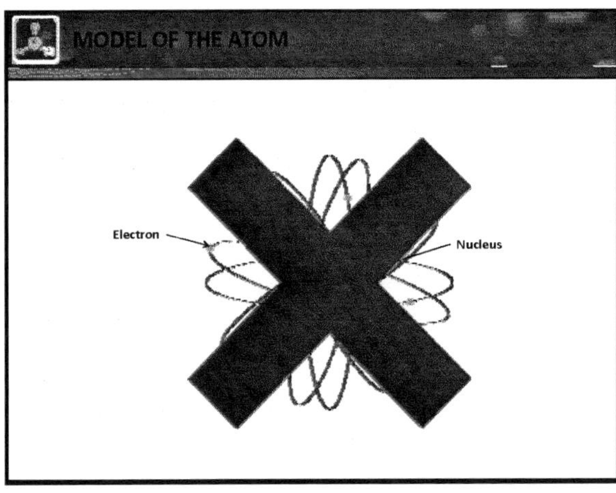
MODEL OF THE ATOM
Electron
Nucleus

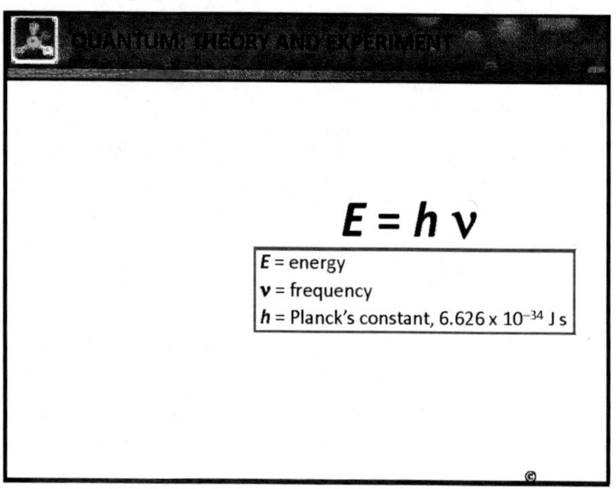
QUANTUM: THEORY AND EXPERIMENT
E = h ν
E = energy
ν = frequency
h = Planck's constant, 6.626 x 10⁻³⁴ J s

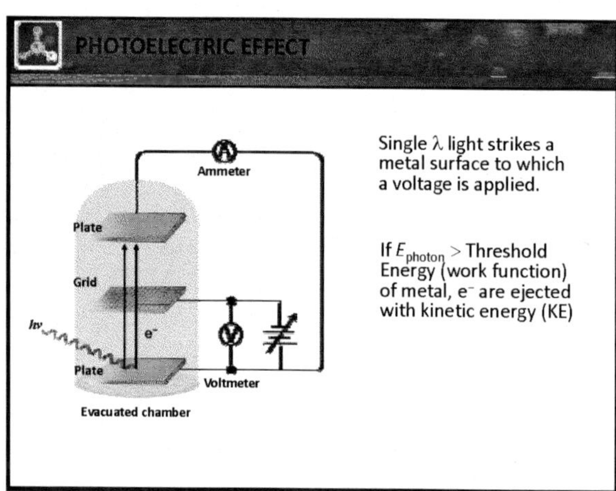
PHOTOELECTRIC EFFECT
Ammeter
Plate
Grid
hν
e⁻
Plate
Voltmeter
Evacuated chamber
Single λ light strikes a metal surface to which a voltage is applied.
If E photon > Threshold Energy (work function) of metal, e⁻ are ejected with kinetic energy (KE)

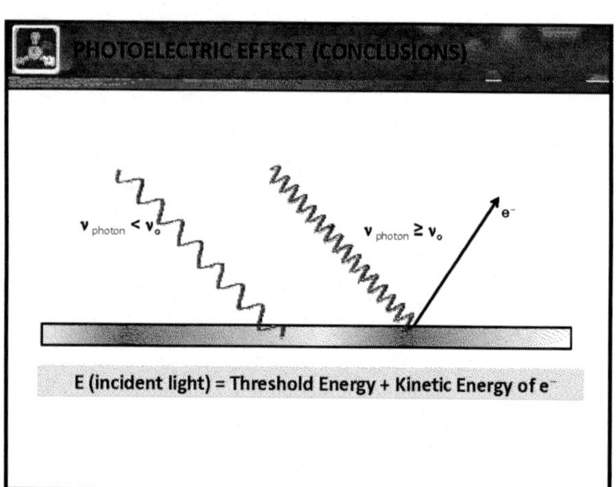
PHOTOELECTRIC EFFECT (CONCLUSIONS)
ν photon < νo
ν photon ≥ νo
e⁻
E (incident light) = Threshold Energy + Kinetic Energy of e⁻

EINSTEIN'S PROPOSAL

KE=½ mu^2

$E=h\nu$

$\nu=c/\lambda$

$E_{photon} = h\nu$

$E = h\nu = hc/\lambda$ = threshold energy + ½ mu^2

PHOTOELECTRIC EFFECT EXAMPLE

Question:

The wavelength of light needed to eject electrons from a metal is 91.2 nm. When light of 80.0nm shines on a sample of the metal, electrons are emitted from the metal.

What is the kinetic energy of each electron, in J?

SOLUTION

The threshold wavelength is 91.2nm.
The incident light is at 80.0 nm.
Watch out for units and use needed conversions (e.g. m and nm).

$$E_{incident\ light} = E_{threshold} + E_{kinetic}$$

$$\frac{hc}{80.0\ \text{nm}} = \frac{hc}{91.2\ \text{nm}} + E_{kinetic}$$

$$E_{kinetic} = hc\left(\frac{1}{80.0\ \text{nm}} - \frac{1}{91.2\ \text{nm}}\right)$$

$$E_{kinetic} = (6.626 \times 10^{-34}\ \text{Js})(2.9979 \times 10^{8}\ \text{ms}^{-1})(10^{9}\ \text{nm m}^{-1})\left(\frac{1}{80.0\ \text{nm}} - \frac{1}{91.2\ \text{nm}}\right)$$

$$E_{kinetic} = 3.030 \times 10^{-19}\ \text{J}$$

CHECKPOINT

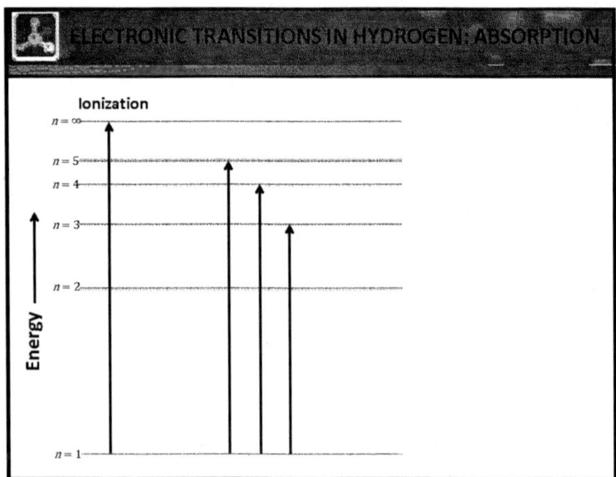
ELECTRONIC TRANSITIONS IN HYDROGEN: ABSORPTION
Ionization
$n = \infty$
$n = 5$
$n = 4$
$n = 3$
$n = 2$
Energy
$n = 1$

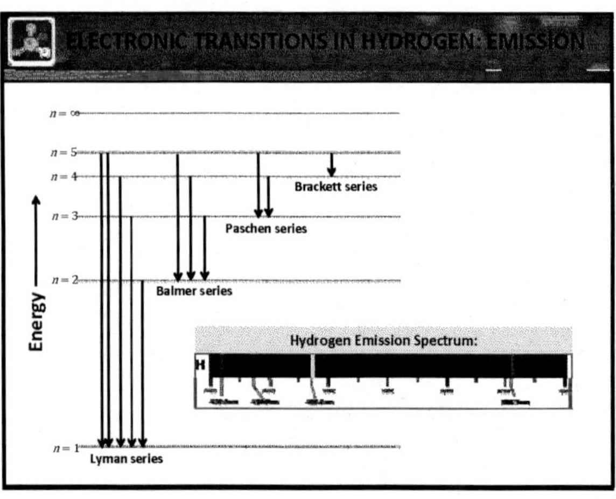
ELECTRONIC TRANSITIONS IN HYDROGEN: EMISSION
$n = \infty$
$n = 5$
$n = 4$
Brackett series
$n = 3$
Paschen series
$n = 2$
Balmer series
Energy
Hydrogen Emission Spectrum:
H
$n = 1$
Lyman series

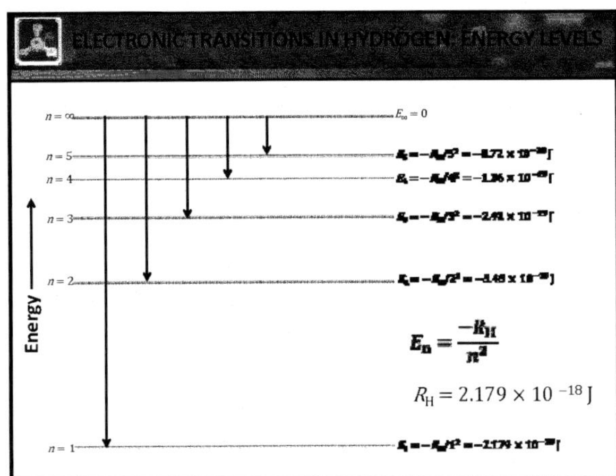

H ATOM ENERGY CHANGES

$$\Delta E = E_f - E_i$$

$$= \frac{-R_H}{n_f^2} - \frac{-R_H}{n_i^2} = R_H\left(\frac{1}{n_i^2} - \frac{1}{n_f^2}\right)$$

ΔE may be positive (absorption) or negative (emission), but $h\nu$ is always positive.

Thus, $h\nu = |\Delta E|$

IONIZATION OF A HYDROGEN ATOM

$$H(g) \longrightarrow H^+(g) + e^-$$

e^- moves from its initial n state (n_i) to a final n state (n_f), where $n_f = \infty$

$$E_f = \frac{-R_H}{n_f^2} = \frac{-R_H}{\infty^2} = 0$$

$$\therefore \Delta E = -E_i$$

EXAMPLE OF A H ATOM CALCULATION

Calculate the wavelength of light required to ionize an H atom from its n=2 state.

$\Delta E = E_f - E_i$ but $E_f = \frac{-R_H}{n_f^2} = \frac{-R_H}{\infty^2} = 0$ $\therefore \Delta E = -E_i$

$\Delta E = -\left(\frac{-R_H}{n_i^2}\right)$

$\Delta E = \left(\frac{2.179 \times 10^{-18}\,\text{J}}{4}\right)$

$\Delta E = 5.448 \times 10^{-19}\,\text{J}$

ANOTHER SAMPLE CALCULATION

Question:

Calculate the frequency of the light emitted when an electron moves from n=2 to n=1 in the H atom.

In what region of the electromagnetic spectrum is this light found?

SOLUTIONS

Frequency of light emitted for n=2 to n=1 transition in H atom:

$\Delta E = E_f - E_i$

$|\Delta E| = h\nu = \frac{-R_H}{n_f^2} - \frac{-R_H}{n_i^2} = R_H\left(\frac{1}{n_i^2} - \frac{1}{n_f^2}\right)$

$\nu = \left|\frac{2.179 \times 10^{-18}\,\text{J}\left(\frac{1}{4} - \frac{1}{1}\right)}{6.626 \times 10^{-34}\,\text{J s}}\right|$

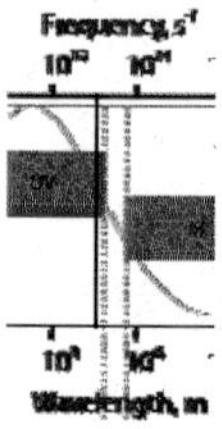

$\nu = 2.466 \times 10^{15}\,\text{s}^{-1}$, in the near ultraviolet region

CHECKPOINT
MODULE 2
Atomic Structure and Theory II
ATOMIC EMISSION VS. ABSORPTION SPECTRA

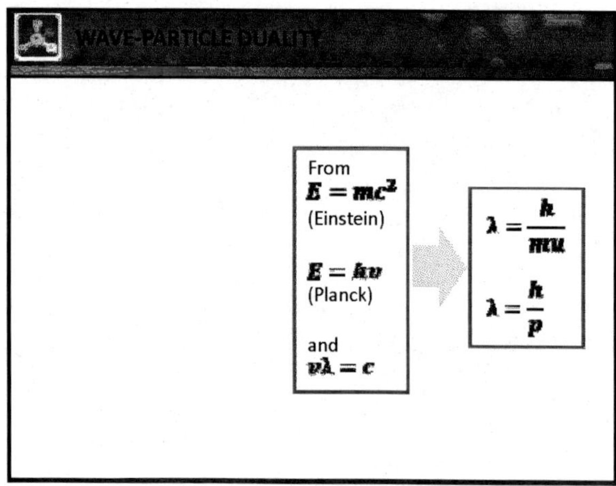
WAVE-PARTICLE DUALITY
From
$E = mc^2$
(Einstein)
$E = h\nu$
(Planck)
and
$\nu\lambda = c$
$\lambda = \frac{h}{mu}$
$\lambda = \frac{h}{p}$

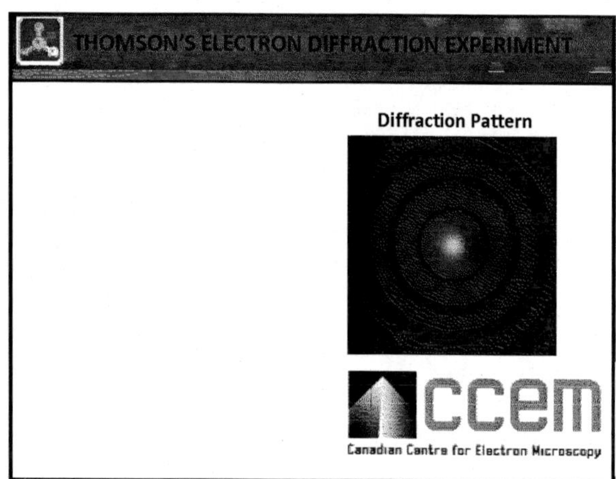
THOMSON'S ELECTRON DIFFRACTION EXPERIMENT
Diffraction Pattern
ccem
Canadian Centre for Electron Microscopy

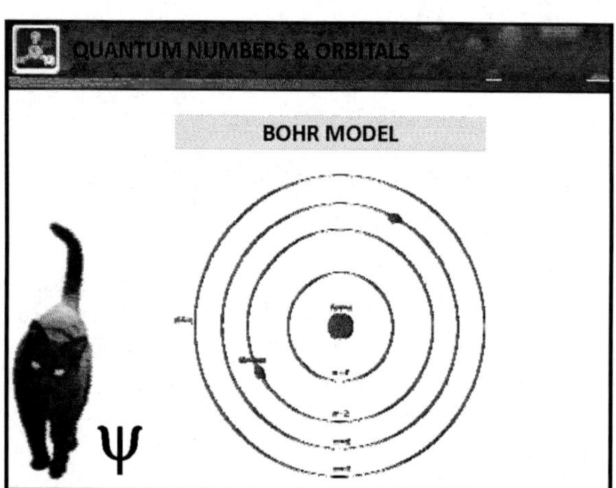
QUANTUM NUMBERS & ORBITALS
BOHR MODEL
ψ

PRINCIPAL QUANTUM NUMBER, n
n
n = ∞
n = 5
n = 4
n = 3
n = 2
Energy
n = 1
n = 3
n = 1, 2, 3, 4, 5, ..., ∞

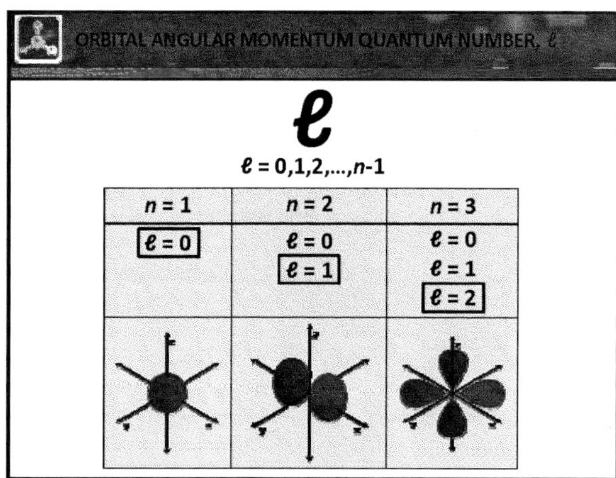
ORBITAL ANGULAR MOMENTUM QUANTUM NUMBER, ℓ
ℓ
ℓ = 0,1,2,...,n-1
n = 1
ℓ = 0
n = 2
ℓ = 0
ℓ = 1
n = 3
ℓ = 0
ℓ = 1
ℓ = 2

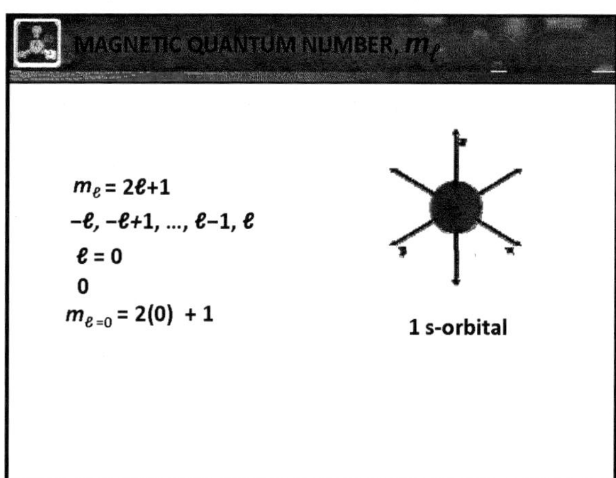
MAGNETIC QUANTUM NUMBER, mℓ
mℓ = 2ℓ+1
−ℓ, −ℓ+1, ..., ℓ−1, ℓ
ℓ = 0
0
mℓ=0 = 2(0) + 1
1 s-orbital

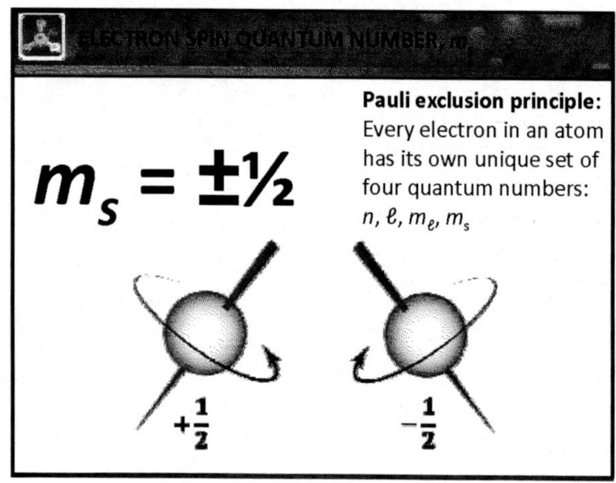
ELECTRON SPIN QUANTUM NUMBER, m_s
Pauli exclusion principle:
Every electron in an atom has its own unique set of four quantum numbers:
n, ℓ, m_ℓ, m_s
$m_s = \pm\frac{1}{2}$
$+\frac{1}{2}$
$-\frac{1}{2}$

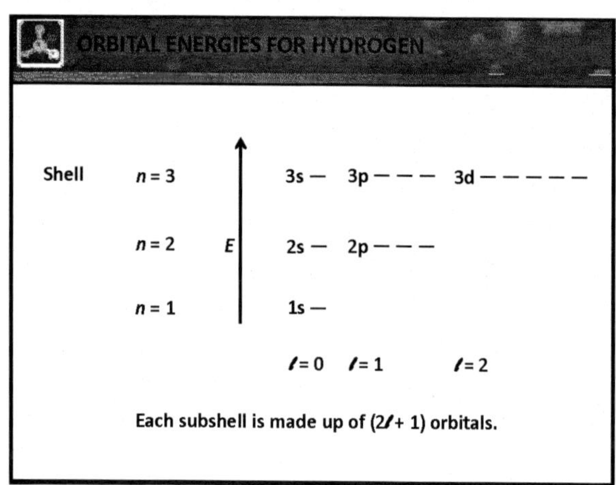
ORBITAL ENERGIES FOR HYDROGEN
Shell
$n = 3$
$n = 2$
$n = 1$
E
3s — 3p — — — 3d — — — — —
2s — 2p — — —
1s —
$\ell = 0$ $\ell = 1$ $\ell = 2$
Each subshell is made up of $(2\ell + 1)$ orbitals.

HYDROGEN VS MULTI-ELECTRON ATOMS

Energy (not to scale)

H	Li
3s 3p 3d	3s 3p 3d
2s 2p	2p
	2s
1s	
	1s

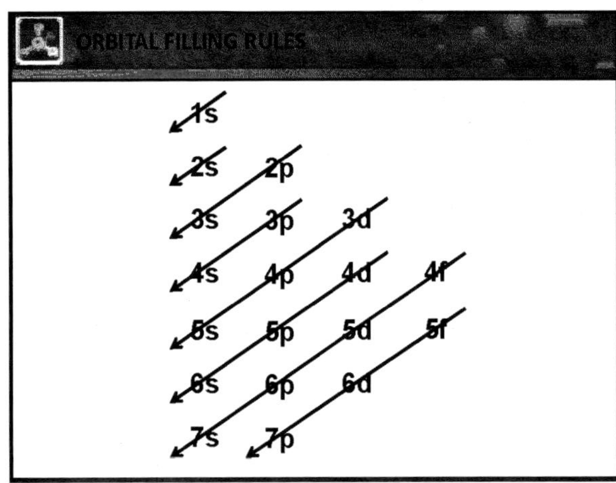

ORBITAL FILLING RULES

CARBON: $1s^2\ 2s^2\ 2p^2$

2p ↑ ↑ __

2s ↑↓

1s ↑↓

THE AUFBAU (BUILDING UP) PROCESS

OXYGEN

2p ↑↓ ↑ ↑

2s ↑↓

1s ↑↓

Oxygen - **Ground State** Electron Configuration: **$1s^22s^22p^4$**

Oxygen - **Noble Gas shorthand: [He] $2s^22p^4$**

CHECKPOINT

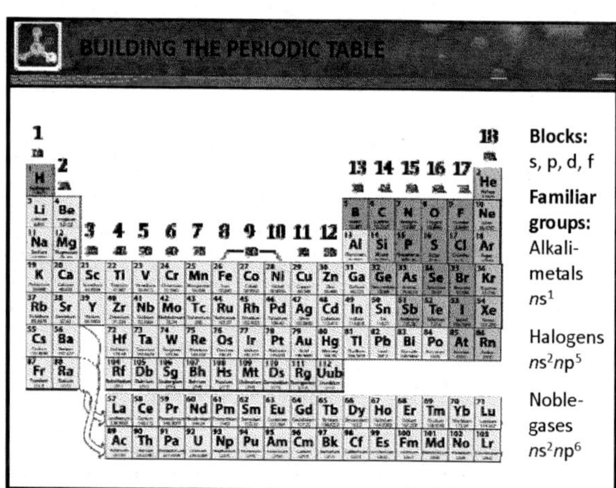
BUILDING THE PERIODIC TABLE
Blocks:
s, p, d, f
Familiar groups:
Alkali-metals
ns1
Halogens
ns2np5
Noble-gases
ns2np6

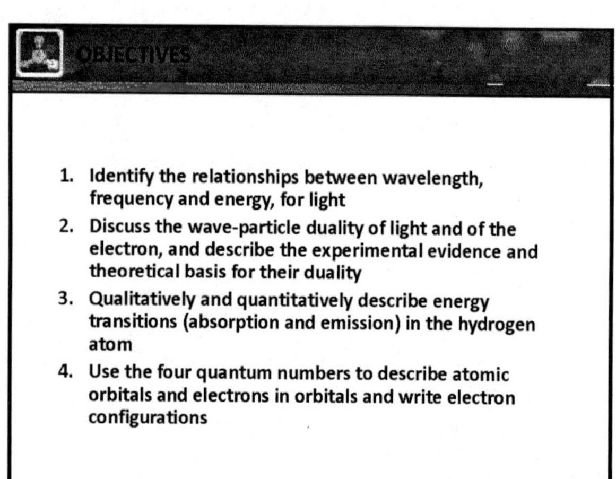
OBJECTIVES
1. Identify the relationships between wavelength, frequency and energy, for light
2. Discuss the wave-particle duality of light and of the electron, and describe the experimental evidence and theoretical basis for their duality
3. Qualitatively and quantitatively describe energy transitions (absorption and emission) in the hydrogen atom
4. Use the four quantum numbers to describe atomic orbitals and electrons in orbitals and write electron configurations

Unit 3

Most important concepts:

-
-
-
-
-
-
-
-
-
-
-
-

Unit 3

Questions I have:

-
-
-
-
-
-
-
-
-
-
-
-

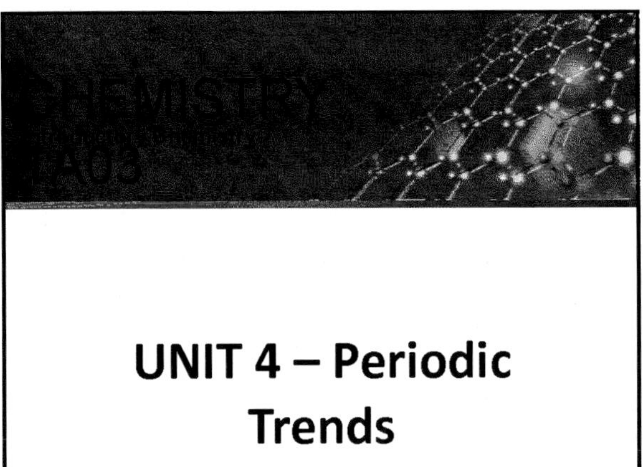
UNIT 4 – Periodic
Trends

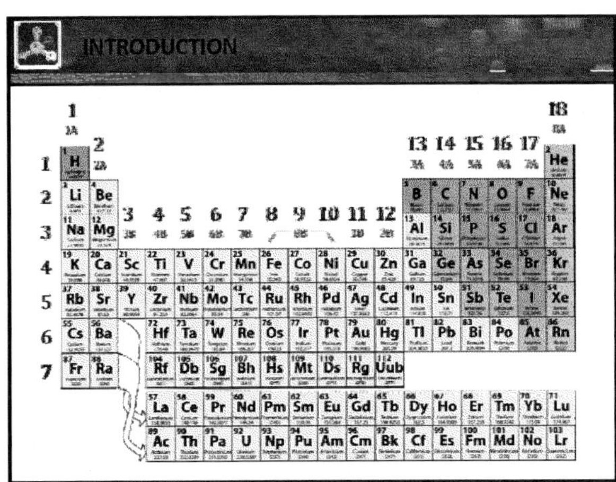
INTRODUCTION

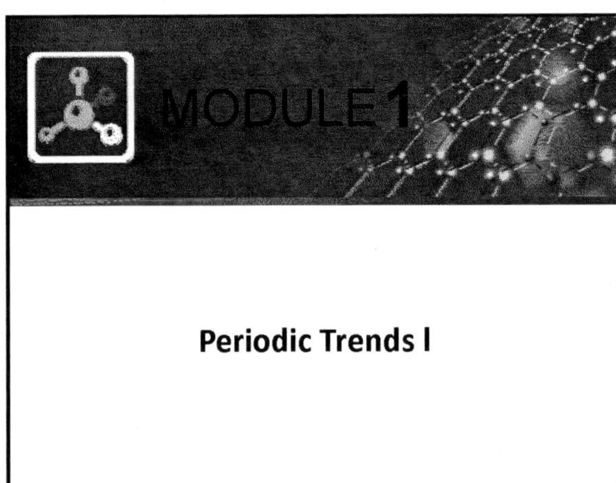
MODULE 1
Periodic Trends I

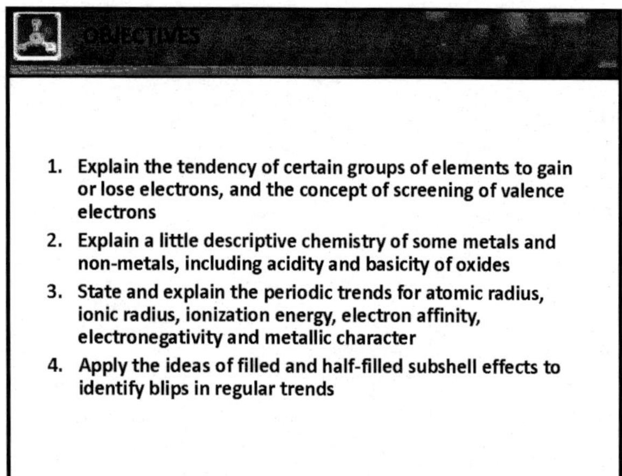
OBJECTIVES
1. Explain the tendency of certain groups of elements to gain or lose electrons, and the concept of screening of valence electrons
2. Explain a little descriptive chemistry of some metals and non-metals, including acidity and basicity of oxides
3. State and explain the periodic trends for atomic radius, ionic radius, ionization energy, electron affinity, electronegativity and metallic character
4. Apply the ideas of filled and half-filled subshell effects to identify blips in regular trends

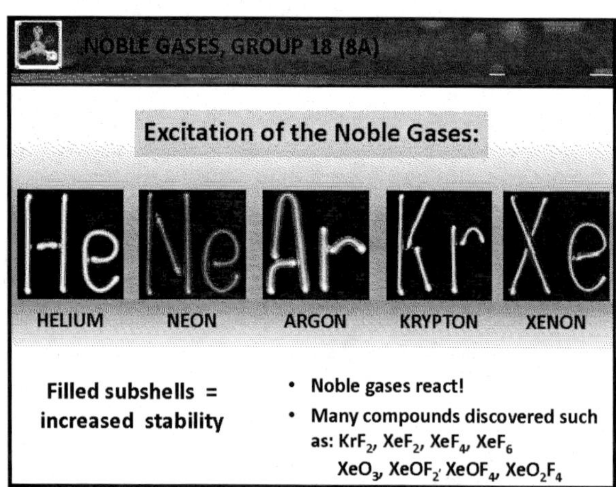
NOBLE GASES, GROUP 18 (8A)
Excitation of the Noble Gases:
HELIUM
NEON
ARGON
KRYPTON
XENON
Filled subshells = increased stability
• Noble gases react!
• Many compounds discovered such as: KrF_2, XeF_2, XeF_4, XeF_6 XeO_3, $XeOF_2$, $XeOF_4$, XeO_2F_4

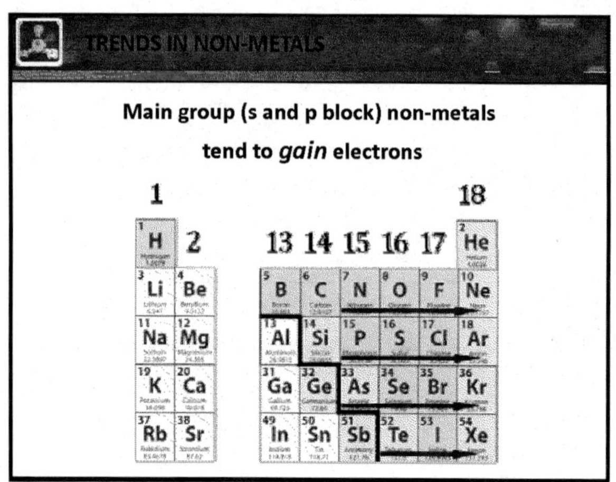
TRENDS IN NON-METALS
Main group (s and p block) non-metals tend to *gain* electrons
1
18
2
13 14 15 16 17
H He
Li Be B C N O F Ne
Na Mg Al Si P S Cl Ar
K Ca Ga Ge As Se Br Kr
Rb Sr In Sn Sb Te I Xe

HALOGENS

NON-METAL OXIDES
SULFUR
S(s) + O2(g) →   (g)

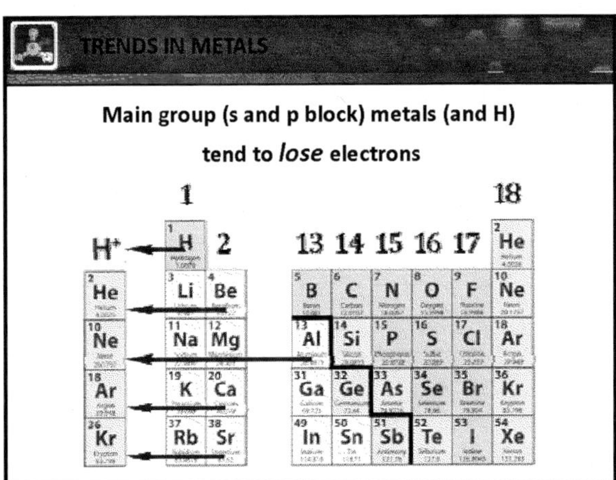
TRENDS IN METALS
Main group (s and p block) metals (and H)
tend to *lose* electrons
1
18
H+
H
2
13 14 15 16 17
He
He
Li Be
B C N O F Ne
Ne
Na Mg
Al Si P S Cl Ar
Ar
K Ca
Ga Ge As Se Br Kr
Kr
Rb Sr
In Sn Sb Te I Xe

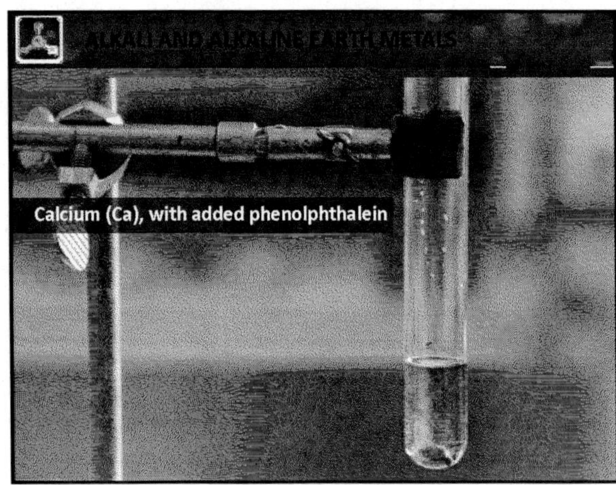
ALKALI AND ALKALINE EARTH METALS
Calcium (Ca), with added phenolphthalein

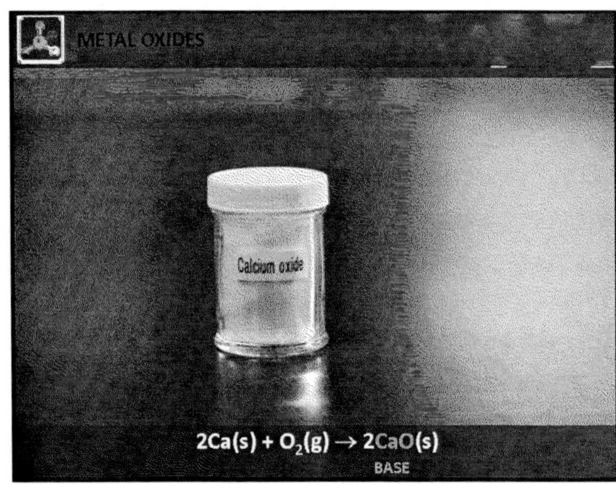
METAL OXIDES
Calcium oxide
$2Ca(s) + O_2(g) \rightarrow 2CaO(s)$
BASE

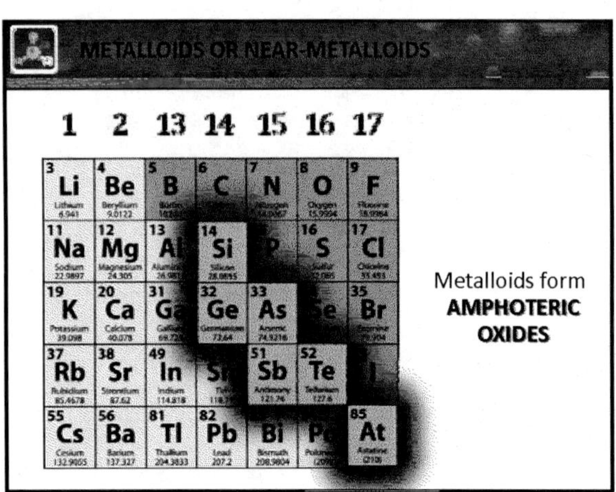
METALLOIDS OR NEAR-METALLOIDS
1 2 13 14 15 16 17
Li Be B C N O F
Na Mg Al Si P S Cl
K Ca Ga Ge As Se Br
Rb Sr In Sn Sb Te I
Cs Ba Tl Pb Bi Po At
Metalloids form
AMPHOTERIC
OXIDES

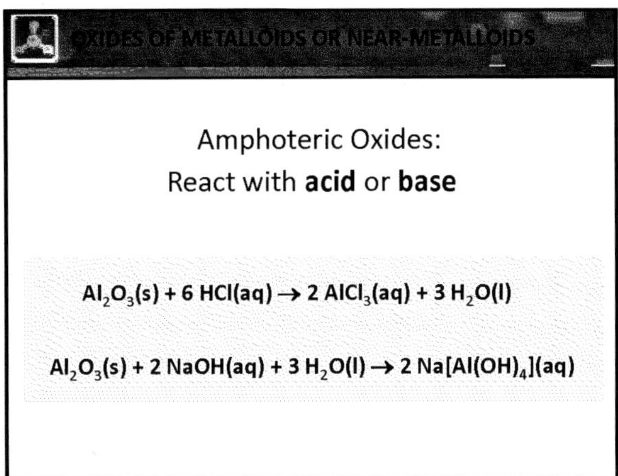
OXIDES OF METALLOIDS OR NEAR-METALLOIDS
Amphoteric Oxides:
React with **acid** or **base**
$Al_2O_3(s) + 6\ HCl(aq) \rightarrow 2\ AlCl_3(aq) + 3\ H_2O(l)$
$Al_2O_3(s) + 2\ NaOH(aq) + 3\ H_2O(l) \rightarrow 2\ Na[Al(OH)_4](aq)$

CHECKPOINT

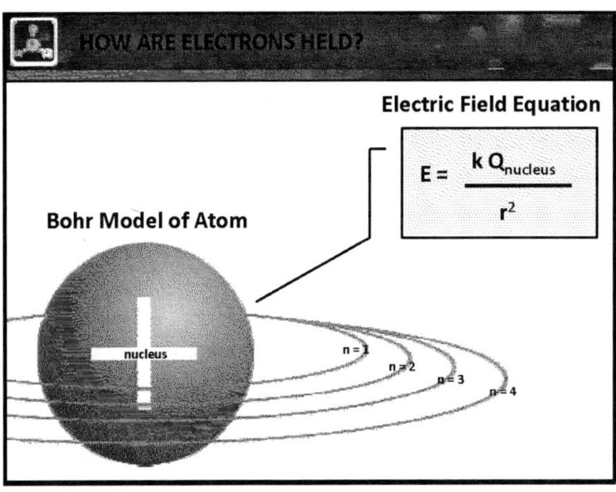
HOW ARE ELECTRONS HELD?
Electric Field Equation
$E = \frac{k\,Q_{nucleus}}{r^2}$
Bohr Model of Atom
nucleus
n = 1
n = 2
n = 3
n = 4

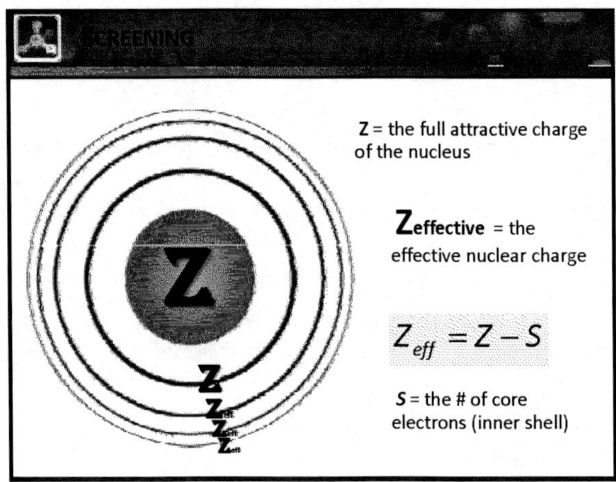

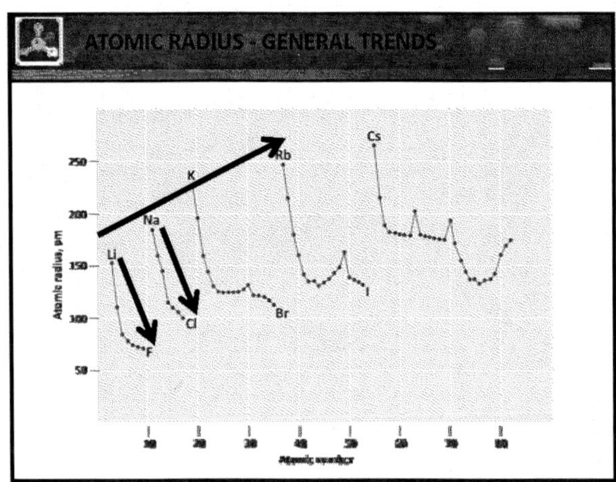

IONIC RADIUS – GENERAL TRENDS

isoelectronic ions = ions with the same number of electrons

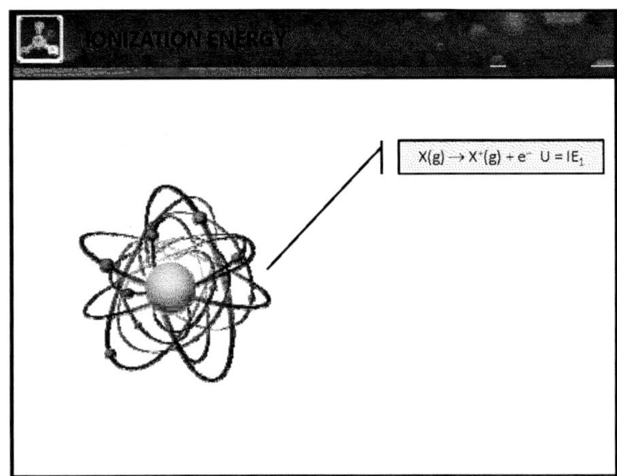
IONIZATION ENERGY
X(g) → X⁺(g) + e⁻ U = IE₁

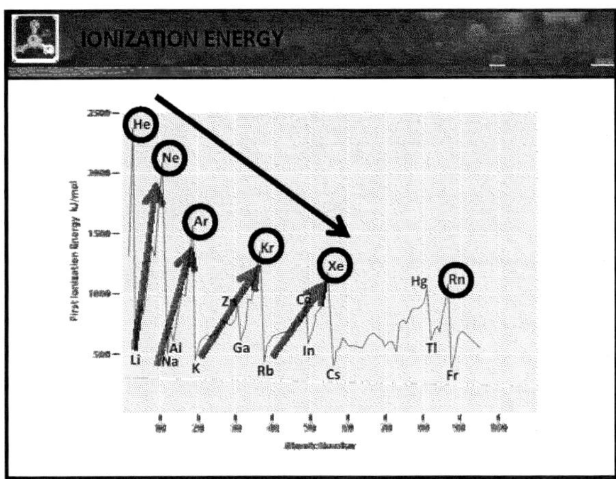
IONIZATION ENERGY
He
Ne
Ar
Kr
Xe
Rn
Hg
Li
Na
Al
K
Ga
Rb
In
Cs
Tl
Fr
First Ionization Energy KJ/mol

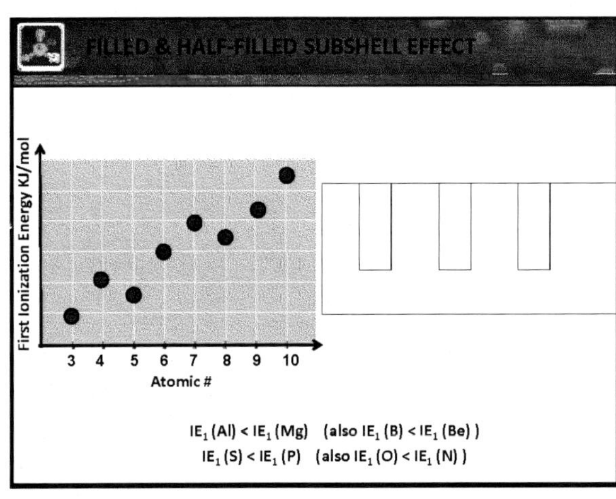
FILLED & HALF-FILLED SUBSHELL EFFECT
First Ionization Energy KJ/mol
3 4 5 6 7 8 9 10
Atomic #
IE₁ (Al) < IE₁ (Mg) (also IE₁ (B) < IE₁ (Be))
IE₁ (S) < IE₁ (P) (also IE₁ (O) < IE₁ (N))

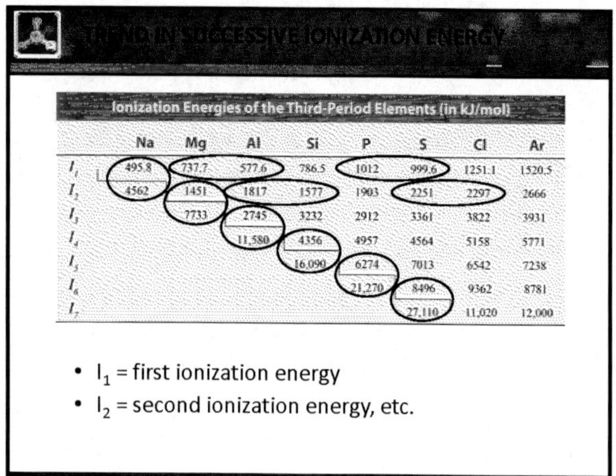

Ionization Energies of the Third-Period Elements (in kJ/mol)

	Na	Mg	Al	Si	P	S	Cl	Ar
I_1	495.8	737.7	577.6	786.5	1012	999.6	1251.1	1520.5
I_2	4562	1451	1817	1577	1903	2251	2297	2666
I_3		7733	2745	3232	2912	3361	3822	3931
I_4			11,580	4356	4957	4564	5158	5771
I_5				16,090	6274	7013	6542	7238
I_6					21,270	8496	9362	8781
I_7						27,110	11,020	12,000

- I_1 = first ionization energy
- I_2 = second ionization energy, etc.

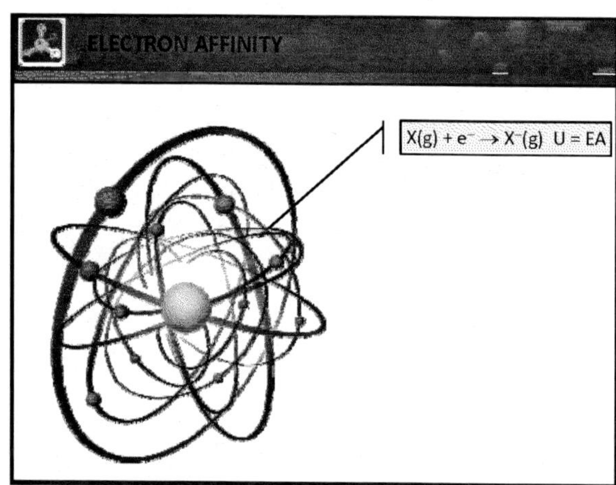

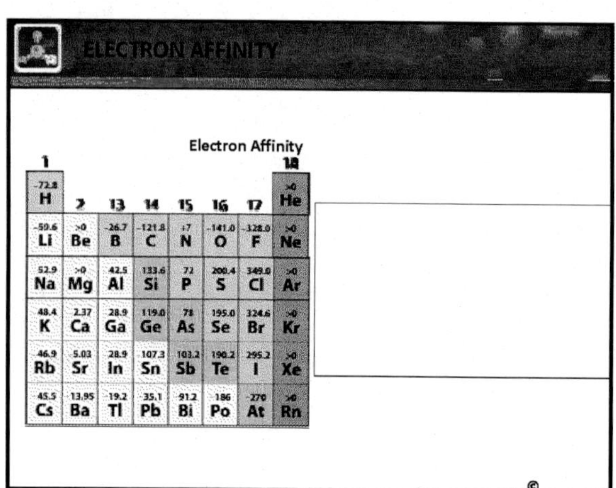

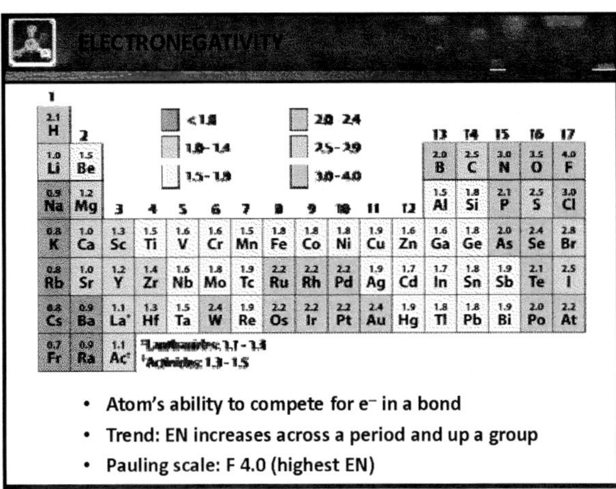
ELECTRONEGATIVITY
Atom's ability to compete for e⁻ in a bond
Trend: EN increases across a period and up a group
Pauling scale: F 4.0 (highest EN)

CHECKPOINT

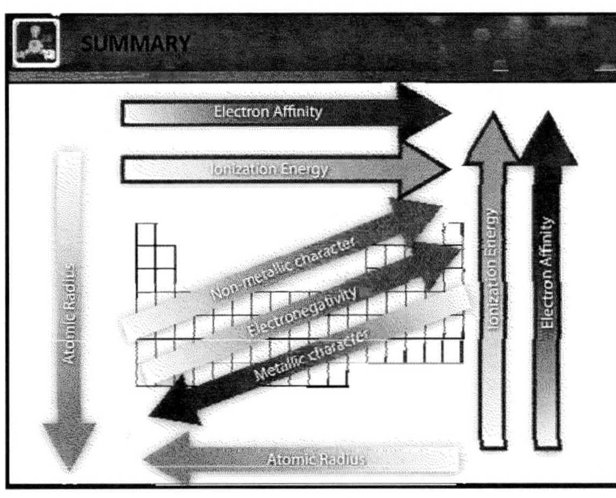
SUMMARY
Electron Affinity
Ionization Energy
Atomic Radius
Non-metallic character
Electronegativity
Metallic character
Ionization Energy
Electron Affinity
Atomic Radius

OBJECTIVES

1. Explain the tendency of certain groups of elements to gain or lose electrons, and the concept of screening of valence electrons
2. Explain a little descriptive chemistry of some metals and non-metals, including acidity and basicity of oxides
3. State and explain the periodic trends for atomic radius, ionic radius, ionization energy, electron affinity, electronegativity and metallic character
4. Apply the ideas of filled and half-filled subshell effects to identify blips in regular trends

Unit 4

Most important concepts:

-
-
-
-
-
-
-
-
-
-
-
-

Unit 4

Questions I have:

-
-
-
-
-
-
-
-
-
-
-
-

UNIT 5 - Chemical Bonding

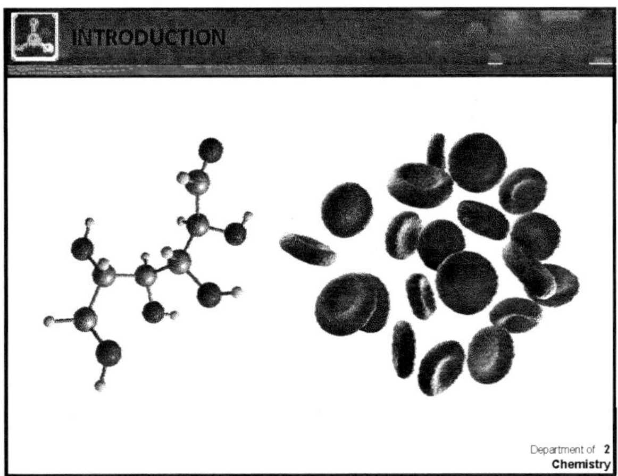

Chemical Bonding I

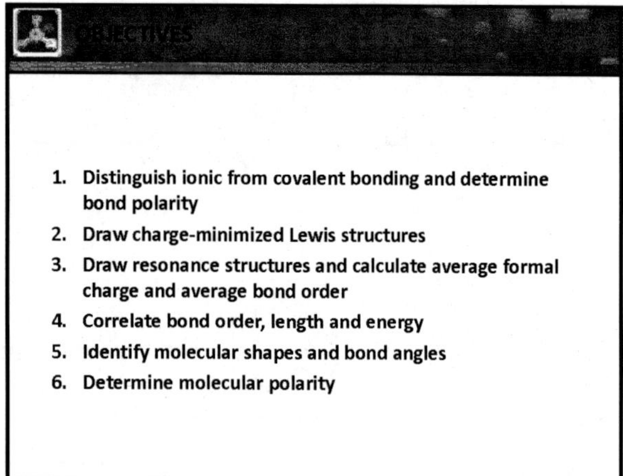

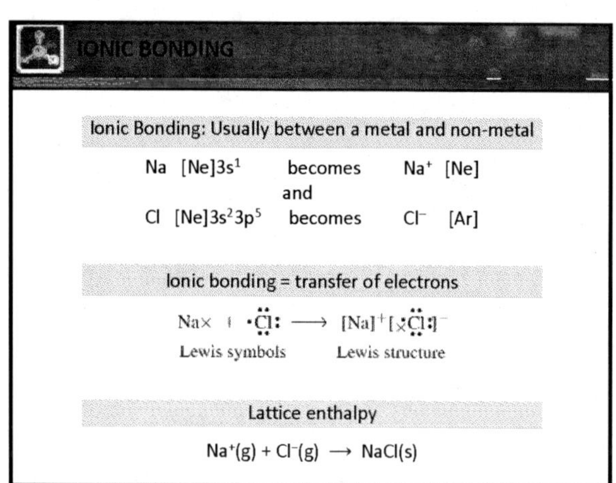

IONIC BONDING
Ionic Bonding: Usually between a metal and non-metal
Na [Ne]3s1 becomes Na+ [Ne]
and
Cl [Ne]3s23p5 becomes Cl− [Ar]
Ionic bonding = transfer of electrons
Na× + ·Cl: ⟶ [Na]+[×Cl:]−
Lewis symbols
Lewis structure
Lattice enthalpy
Na+(g) + Cl−(g) ⟶ NaCl(s)

COVALENT BONDING

- **Covalent bond**
  - e^- are shared between two atoms
- **Coordinate covalent bond**
  - One atom provides both e^- for a bond
  - e.g. $NH_3 + H^+ \rightarrow NH_4^+$

$$\mathrm{H{:}\ddot{N}{:}H\ (H\ above,\ H\ below)} + H^+ \longrightarrow [\mathrm{H{:}\ddot{N}{:}H\ (H\ above,\ H\ below)}]^+$$

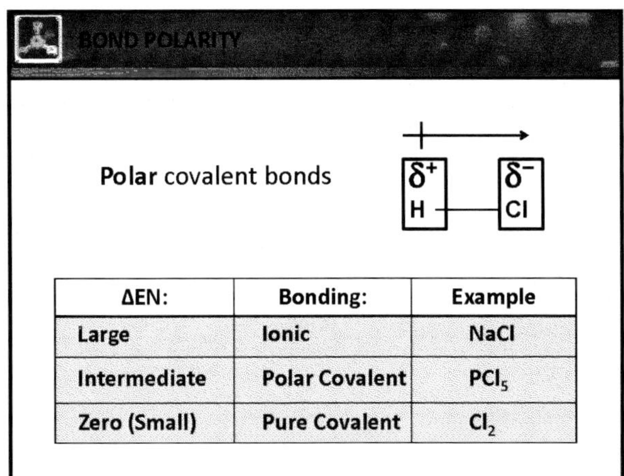

ΔEN:	Bonding:	Example
Large	Ionic	NaCl
Intermediate	Polar Covalent	PCl_5
Zero (Small)	Pure Covalent	Cl_2

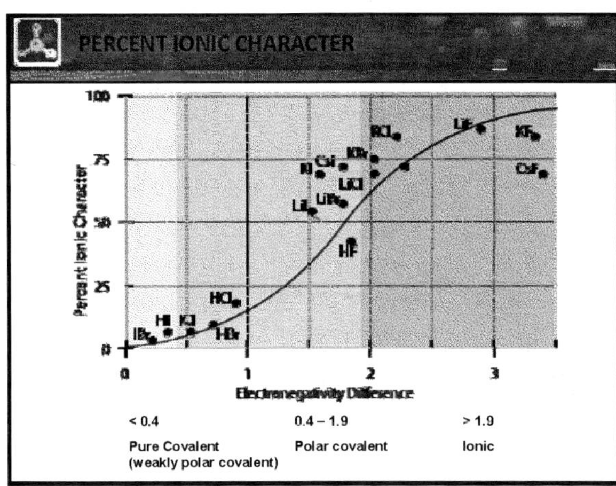

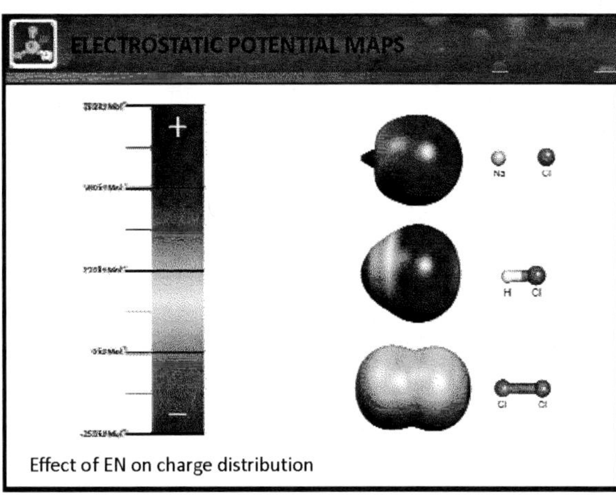

Effect of EN on charge distribution

CHECKPOINT

LEWIS STRUCTURES

- Show bonding (b) and non-bonding (nb) e^-, and formal charges
- Octet* can be achieved by combination of bonding and nonbonding e^-
  *(not all atoms will have an octet)
- Bonding e^- can be single, double, triple bonds

RULES FOR DRAWING LEWIS STRUCTURES

1. Count total # of e^- (include charge)
   - Add e^- for negative charge, subtract e^- for positive charge
2. Draw skeletal structure (central & terminal atoms)
   - The least electronegative atom is generally the central atom
   - H and F are always terminal
3. Deduct 2 e^- for each single bond of skeleton
4. Use remaining e^- to complete octet of terminal atoms
   - Only 2 e^- for H
5. Subtract e^- used for terminal octets
6. If e^- remain, place on central atom

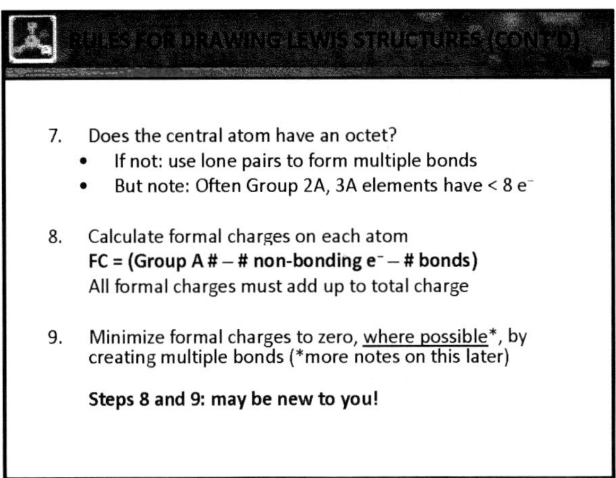
RULES FOR DRAWING LEWIS STRUCTURES (CONT'D)
7. Does the central atom have an octet?
• If not: use lone pairs to form multiple bonds
• But note: Often Group 2A, 3A elements have < 8 e⁻
8. Calculate formal charges on each atom
FC = (Group A # – # non-bonding e⁻ – # bonds)
All formal charges must add up to total charge
9. Minimize formal charges to zero, where possible*, by creating multiple bonds (*more notes on this later)
Steps 8 and 9: may be new to you!

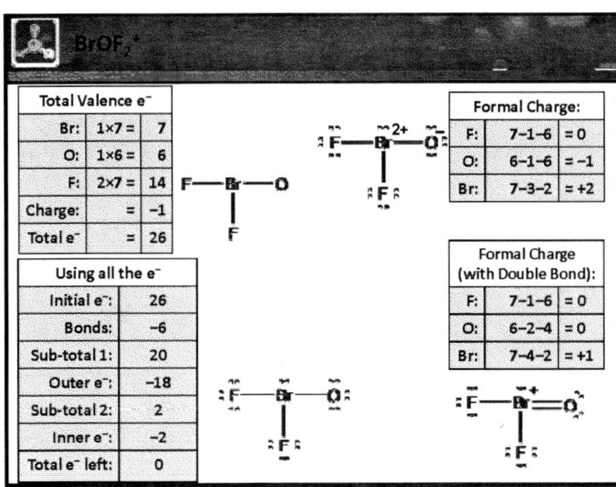
BrOF2+
Total Valence e⁻
Br: 1×7 = 7
O: 1×6 = 6
F: 2×7 = 14
Charge: = -1
Total e⁻ = 26
Using all the e⁻
Initial e⁻: 26
Bonds: -6
Sub-total 1: 20
Outer e⁻: -18
Sub-total 2: 2
Inner e⁻: -2
Total e⁻ left: 0
F
Br
O
2+
Formal Charge:
F: 7–1–6 = 0
O: 6–1–6 = -1
Br: 7–3–2 = +2
Formal Charge (with Double Bond):
F: 7–1–6 = 0
O: 6–2–4 = 0
Br: 7–4–2 = +1
+

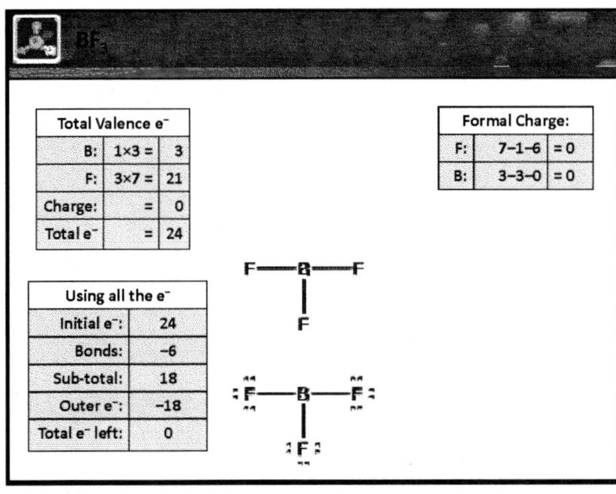
BF3
Total Valence e⁻
B: 1×3 = 3
F: 3×7 = 21
Charge: = 0
Total e⁻ = 24
Using all the e⁻
Initial e⁻: 24
Bonds: -6
Sub-total: 18
Outer e⁻: -18
Total e⁻ left: 0
F
B
Formal Charge:
F: 7–1–6 = 0
B: 3–3–0 = 0

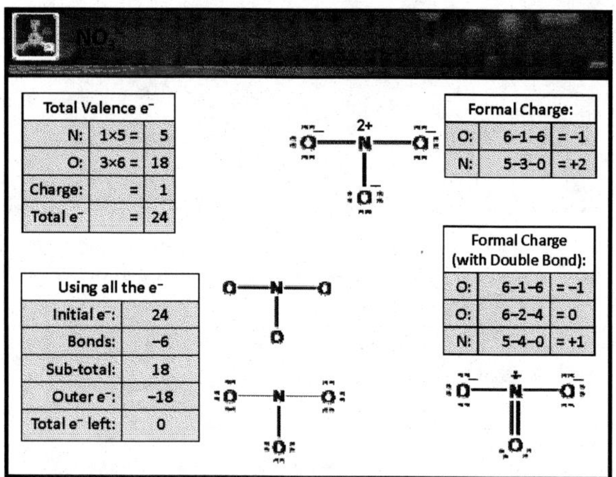

NOTES ABOUT LEWIS STRUCTURES

- Octet is not exceeded in Period 2
  - C N O F can not over fill
- Periods 3, 4, etc.: minimize formal charges, even if it means breaking the "octet rule".
- adjacent atoms rarely have same formal charge
- ***usually*** negative charges on electronegative atoms and positive charges on electropositive atoms

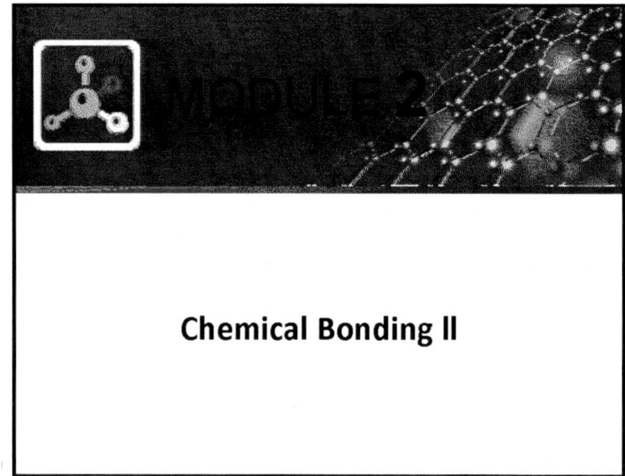
MODULE 2
Chemical Bonding II

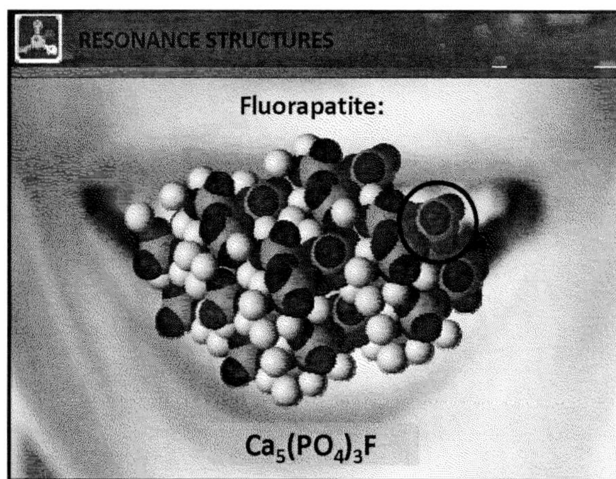
RESONANCE STRUCTURES
Fluorapatite:
Ca5(PO4)3F

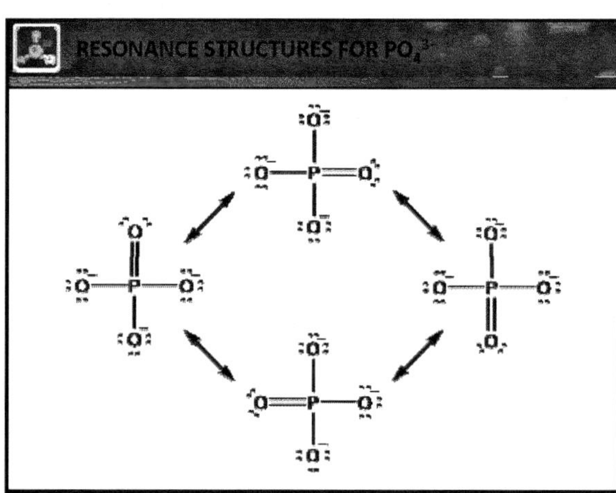
RESONANCE STRUCTURES FOR PO4 3-

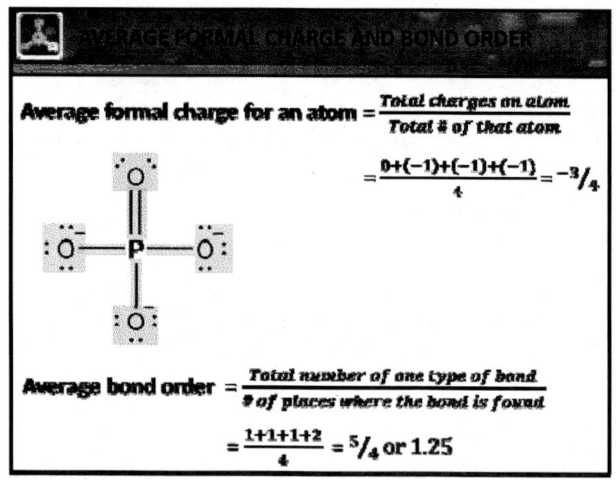

AVERAGE FORMAL CHARGE AND BOND ORDER
Average formal charge for an atom = Total charges on atom / Total # of that atom
= (0+(−1)+(−1)+(−1)) / 4 = −3/4
Average bond order = Total number of one type of bond / # of places where the bond is found
= (1+1+1+2) / 4 = 5/4 or 1.25

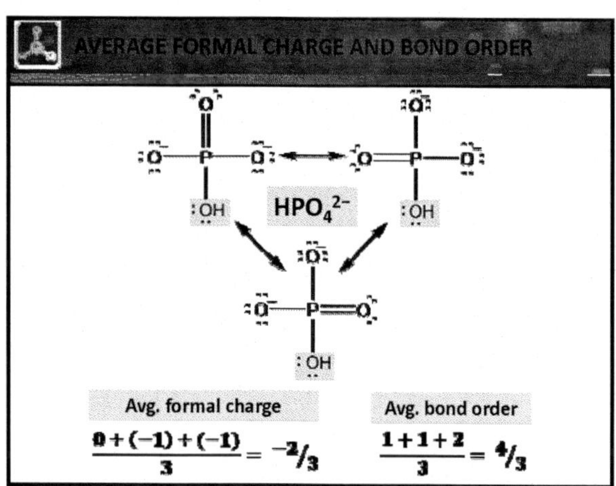

BOND ORDER, LENGTH, & ENERGY

Bond order:

single (1)	double (2)	triple (3)
M−M	M=M	M≡M

Covalent bond length

H—H
74.14 pm

- Approximately the sum of covalent radii
- Diatomic molecules allow precise values; other values are averages

Bond dissociation energy, *D*

- Energy required to break 1 mol of bonds in **gas phase**
- Diatomic molecules allow precise values; other values are averages

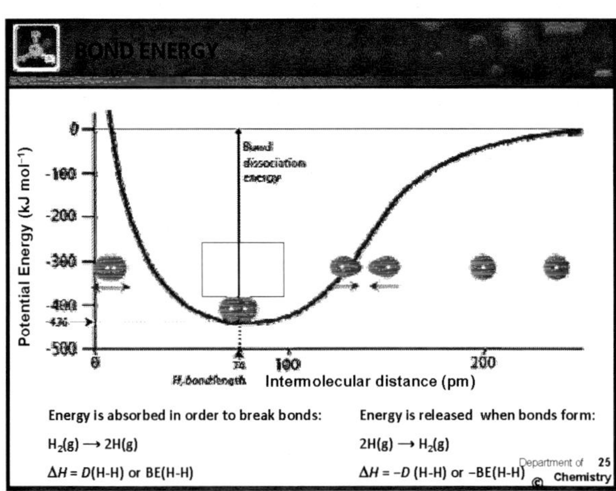

BOND ORDER, LENGTH, AND ENERGY

Bond	Order	Length, pm	Energy, kJ mol^{-1}
C—C	1	154	347
C=C	2	134	611
C≡C	3	120	837
N≡N	3	109.8	946

CHECKPOINT

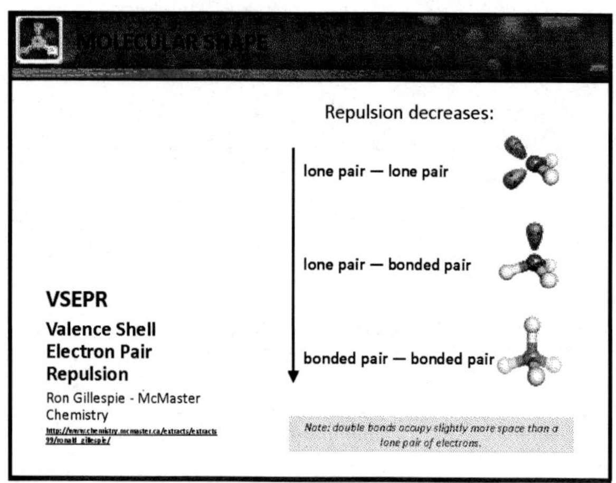
MOLECULAR SHAPE
Repulsion decreases:
lone pair — lone pair
lone pair — bonded pair
bonded pair — bonded pair
VSEPR
Valence Shell
Electron Pair
Repulsion
Ron Gillespie - McMaster
Chemistry
Note: double bonds occupy slightly more space than a lone pair of electrons.

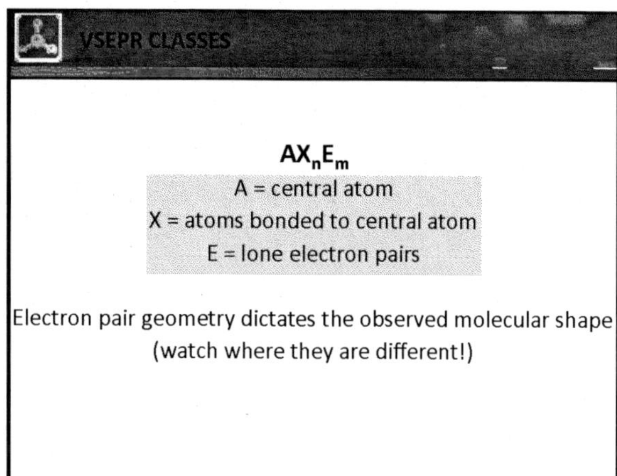
VSEPR CLASSES
AX_nE_m
A = central atom
X = atoms bonded to central atom
E = lone electron pairs
Electron pair geometry dictates the observed molecular shape
(watch where they are different!)

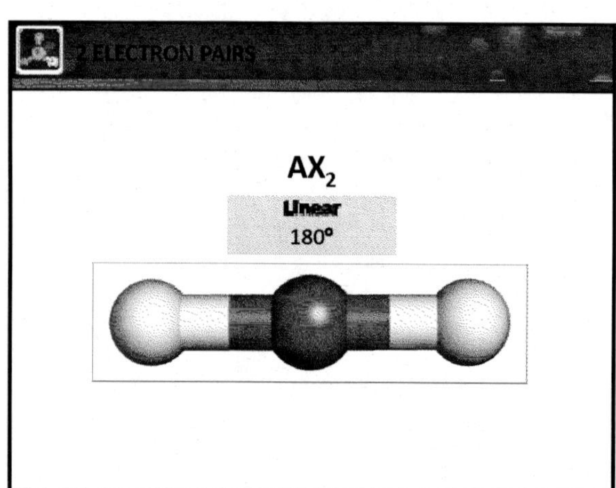
2 ELECTRON PAIRS
AX_2
Linear
180°

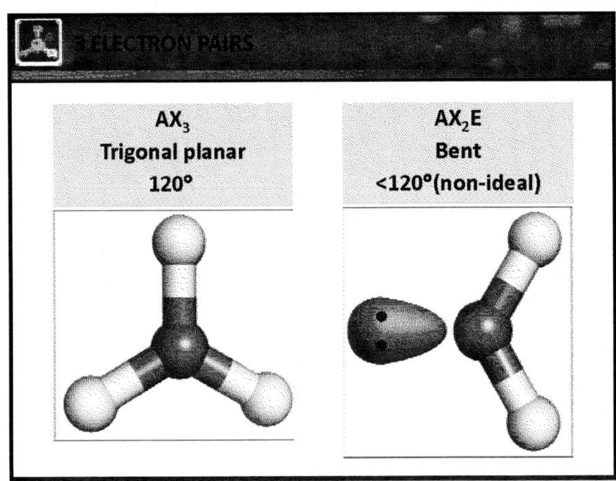
3 ELECTRON PAIRS
AX_3
Trigonal planar
120°
AX_2E
Bent
<120°(non-ideal)

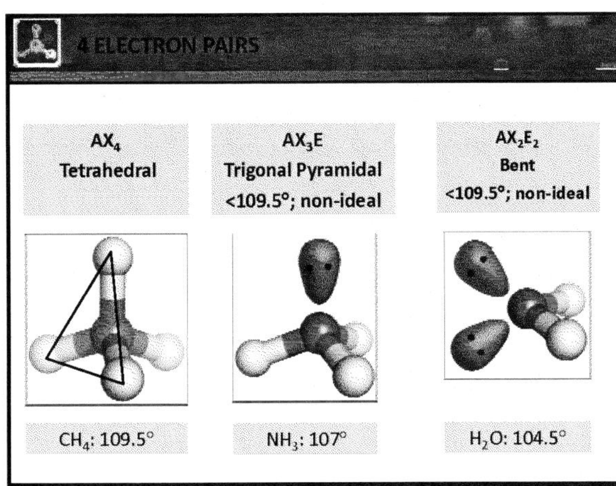
4 ELECTRON PAIRS
AX_4
Tetrahedral
AX_3E
Trigonal Pyramidal
<109.5°; non-ideal
AX_2E_2
Bent
<109.5°; non-ideal
CH_4: 109.5°
NH_3: 107°
H_2O: 104.5°

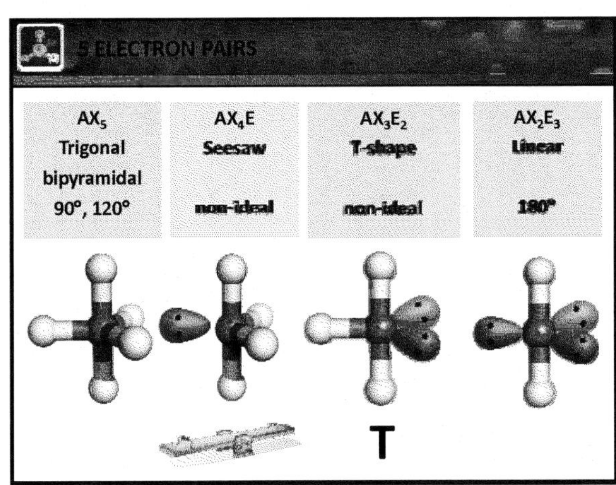
5 ELECTRON PAIRS
AX_5
Trigonal
bipyramidal
90°, 120°
AX_4E
Seesaw
non-ideal
AX_3E_2
T-shape
non-ideal
AX_2E_3
Linear
180°
T

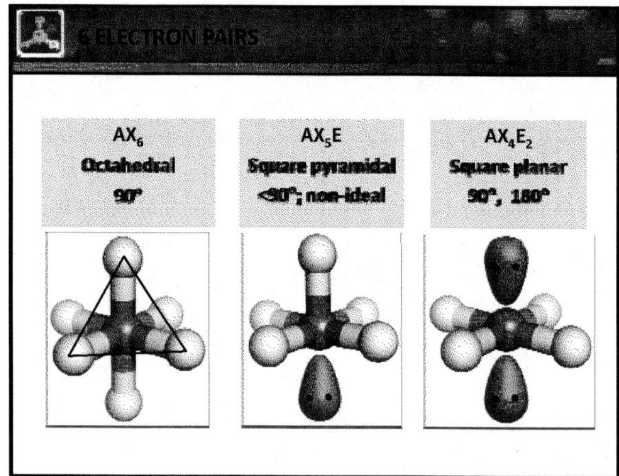
6 ELECTRON PAIRS
AX6
Octahedral
90°
AX5E
Square pyramidal
<90°; non-ideal
AX4E2
Square planar
90°, 180°

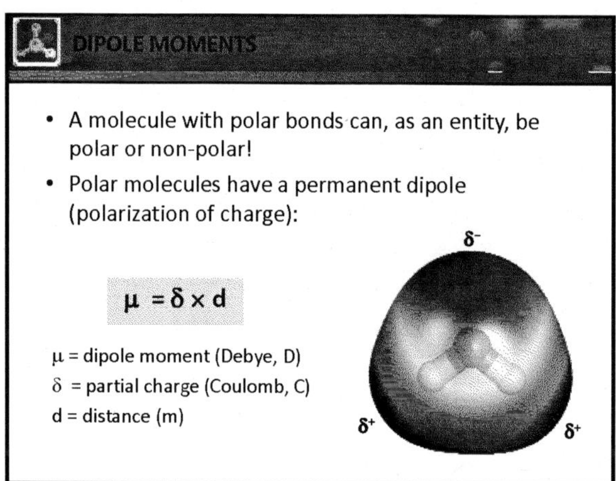
DIPOLE MOMENTS
A molecule with polar bonds can, as an entity, be polar or non-polar!
Polar molecules have a permanent dipole (polarization of charge):
μ = δ x d
μ = dipole moment (Debye, D)
δ = partial charge (Coulomb, C)
d = distance (m)
δ-
δ+
δ+

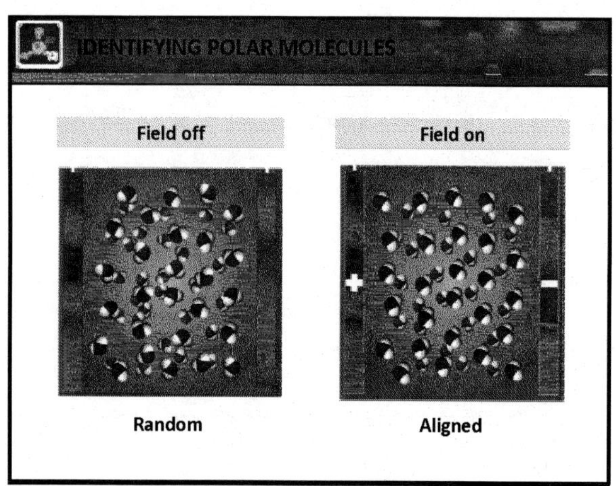
IDENTIFYING POLAR MOLECULES
Field off
Field on
Random
Aligned

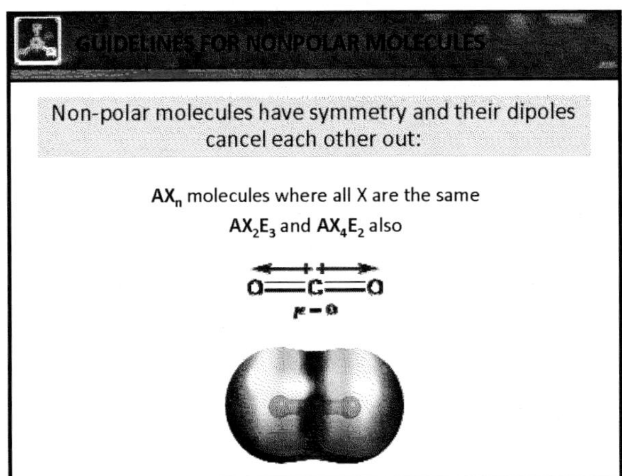
GUIDELINES FOR NONPOLAR MOLECULES
Non-polar molecules have symmetry and their dipoles cancel each other out:
AX$_n$ molecules where all X are the same
AX$_2$E$_3$ and AX$_4$E$_2$ also
O=C=O
μ = 0

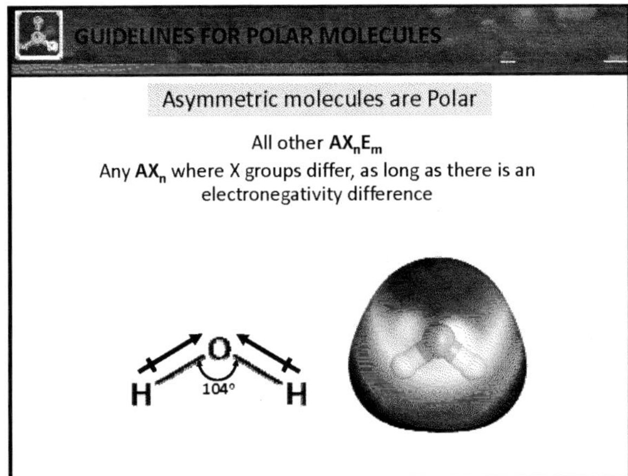
GUIDELINES FOR POLAR MOLECULES
Asymmetric molecules are Polar
All other AX$_n$E$_m$
Any AX$_n$ where X groups differ, as long as there is an electronegativity difference
O
H
H
104°

CHECKPOINT

OBJECTIVES

1. Distinguish ionic from covalent bonding and determine bond polarity
2. Draw charge-minimized Lewis structures
3. Draw resonance structures and calculate average formal charge and average bond order
4. Correlate bond order, length and energy
5. Identify molecular shapes and bond angles
6. Determine molecular polarity

Unit 5

Most important concepts:

-
-
-
-
-
-
-
-
-
-
-
-

Unit 5

Questions I have:

-
-
-
-
-
-
-
-
-
-
-
-

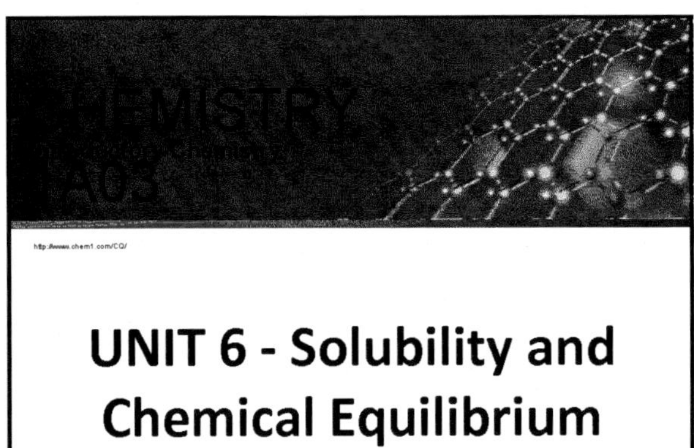
UNIT 6 - Solubility and
Chemical Equilibrium

INTRODUCTION

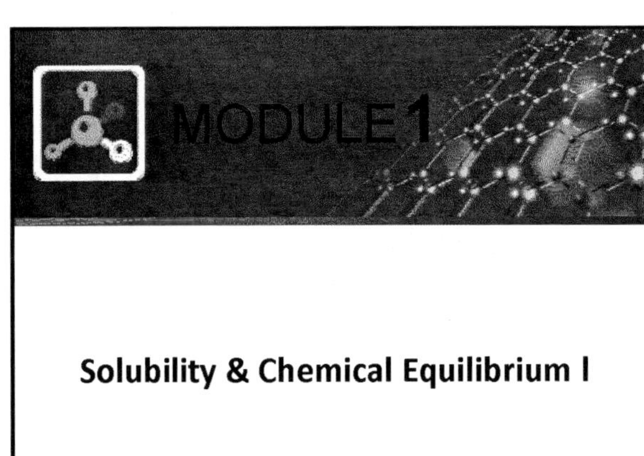
MODULE 1
Solubility & Chemical Equilibrium I

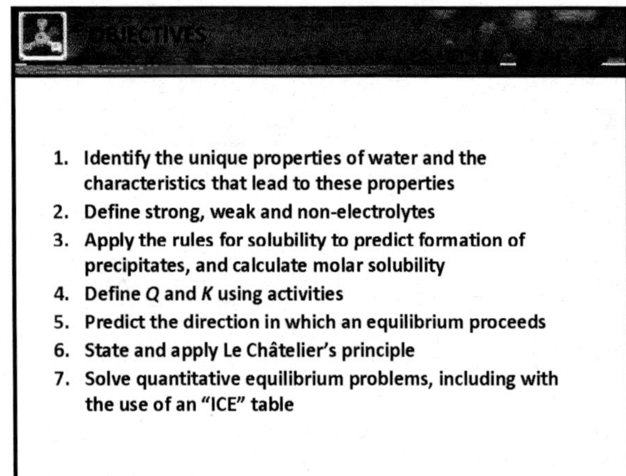
OBJECTIVES
1. Identify the unique properties of water and the characteristics that lead to these properties
2. Define strong, weak and non-electrolytes
3. Apply the rules for solubility to predict formation of precipitates, and calculate molar solubility
4. Define Q and K using activities
5. Predict the direction in which an equilibrium proceeds
6. State and apply Le Châtelier's principle
7. Solve quantitative equilibrium problems, including with the use of an "ICE" table

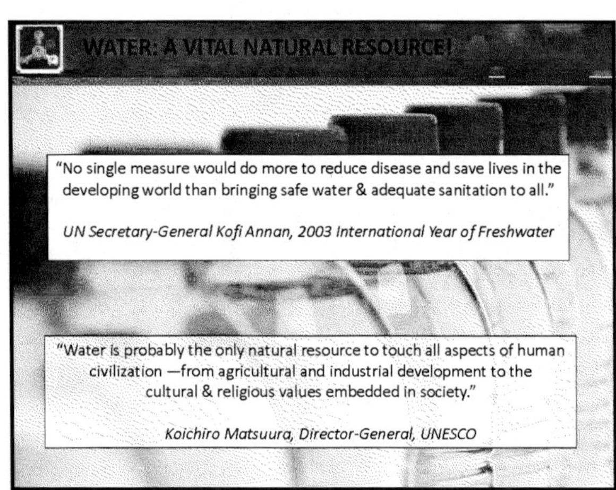
WATER: A VITAL NATURAL RESOURCE!
"No single measure would do more to reduce disease and save lives in the developing world than bringing safe water & adequate sanitation to all."
UN Secretary-General Kofi Annan, 2003 International Year of Freshwater
"Water is probably the only natural resource to touch all aspects of human civilization —from agricultural and industrial development to the cultural & religious values embedded in society."
Koichiro Matsuura, Director-General, UNESCO

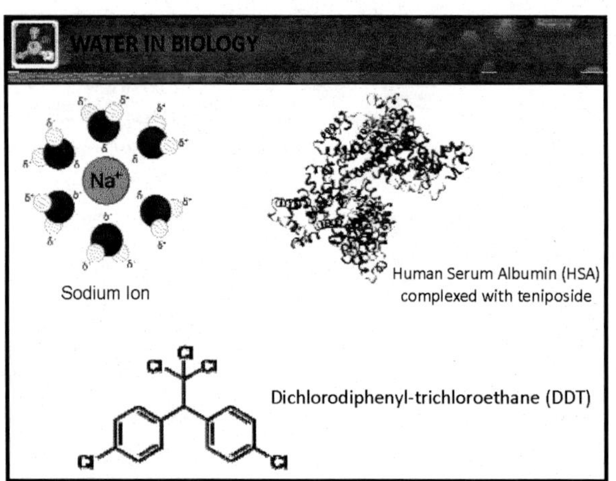
WATER IN BIOLOGY
Na+
Sodium Ion
Human Serum Albumin (HSA) complexed with teniposide
Dichlorodiphenyl-trichloroethane (DDT)

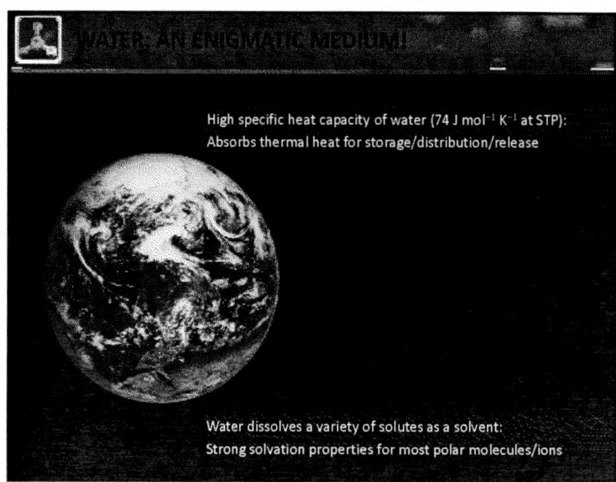
WATER: AN ENIGMATIC MEDIUM!
High specific heat capacity of water (74 J mol⁻¹ K⁻¹ at STP):
Absorbs thermal heat for storage/distribution/release
Water dissolves a variety of solutes as a solvent:
Strong solvation properties for most polar molecules/ions

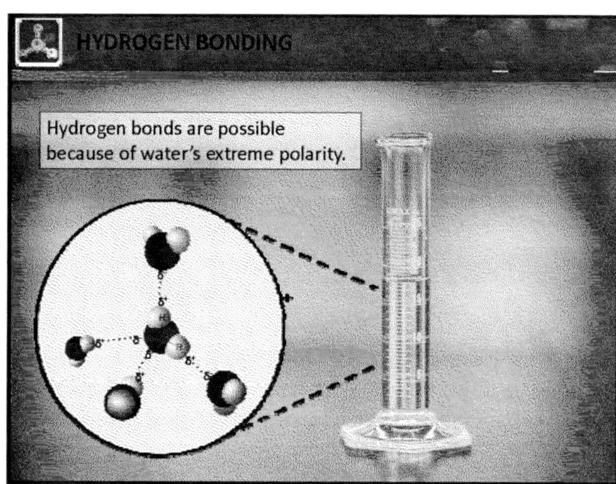
HYDROGEN BONDING
Hydrogen bonds are possible
because of water's extreme polarity.

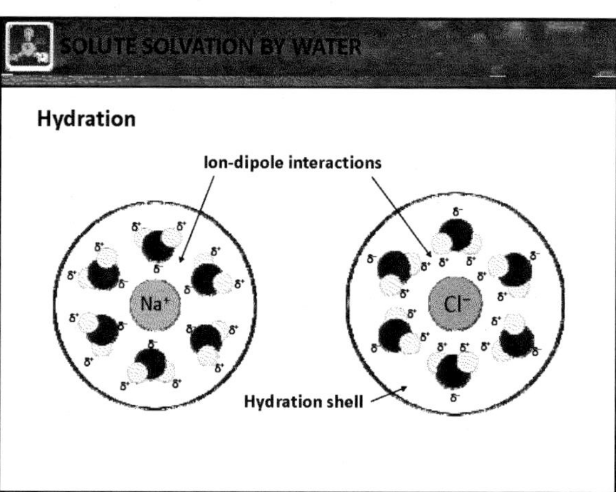
SOLUTE SOLVATION BY WATER
Hydration
Ion-dipole interactions
Na⁺
Cl⁻
Hydration shell

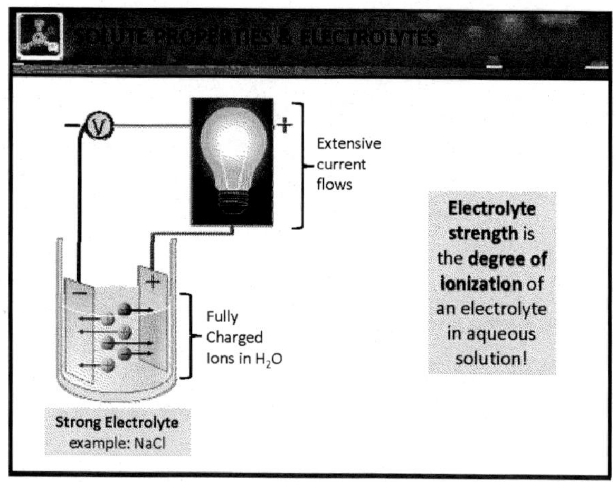
SOLUTE PROPERTIES & ELECTROLYTES
V
Extensive current flows
Fully Charged Ions in H_2O
Strong Electrolyte example: NaCl
Electrolyte strength is the **degree of ionization** of an electrolyte in aqueous solution!

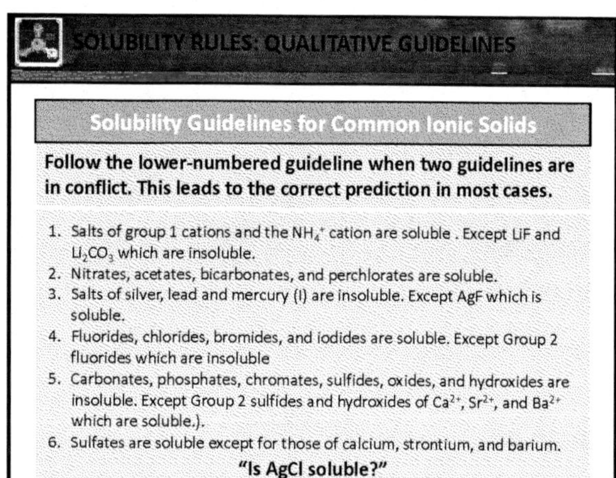
SOLUBILITY RULES: QUALITATIVE GUIDELINES
Solubility Guidelines for Common Ionic Solids
Follow the lower-numbered guideline when two guidelines are in conflict. This leads to the correct prediction in most cases.
1. Salts of group 1 cations and the NH_4^+ cation are soluble . Except LiF and Li_2CO_3 which are insoluble.
2. Nitrates, acetates, bicarbonates, and perchlorates are soluble.
3. Salts of silver, lead and mercury (I) are insoluble. Except AgF which is soluble.
4. Fluorides, chlorides, bromides, and iodides are soluble. Except Group 2 fluorides which are insoluble
5. Carbonates, phosphates, chromates, sulfides, oxides, and hydroxides are insoluble. Except Group 2 sulfides and hydroxides of Ca^{2+}, Sr^{2+}, and Ba^{2+} which are soluble.).
6. Sulfates are soluble except for those of calcium, strontium, and barium.
"Is AgCl soluble?"

CHECKPOINT

NET IONIC REACTION

Precipitation of AgI (s)

$AgNO_3$ (aq) + KI (aq) ⟶ AgI (s) + KNO_3 (aq)

or

Total Ionic Equation

Ag^+ (aq) + NO_3^- (aq) + K^+ (aq) + I^- (aq) ⟶ AgI (s) + K^+ (aq) + NO_3^- (aq)

Spectator Ions Derived from Strong Electrolytes

Net Ionic Equation: Ag^+ (aq) + I^- (aq) ⟶ AqI (s)

NUMERICAL EXAMPLE

Determine the mass of KI needed to precipitate 0.1 mM of $AgNO_3$ in a 20 mL sample solution.

Balanced equation:
$AgNO_3$ (aq) + KI (aq) → AgI (s) + KNO_3(aq)

Moles of $AgNO_3$ present in solution:
$(1 \times 10^{-4}$ mol $L^{-1}) \times (2 \times 10^{-2}$ L$) = 2 \times 10^{-6}$ moles of $AgNO_3$

moles of KI = moles of $AgNO_3$, from the balanced reaction.

Mass of KI = 2×10^{-6} moles × 166.0 g mol^{-1} = 0.3 mg

CHECKPOINT

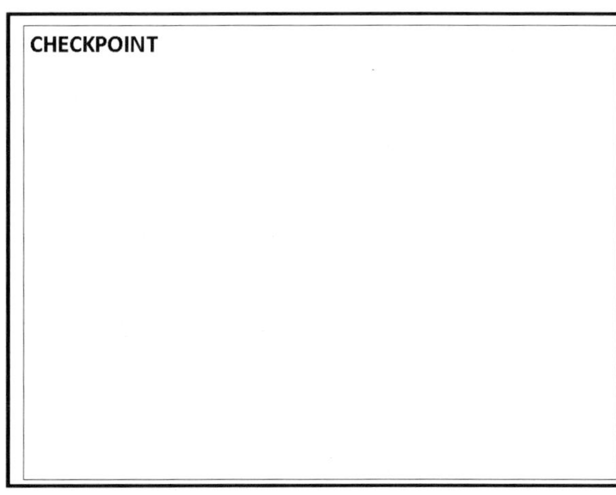

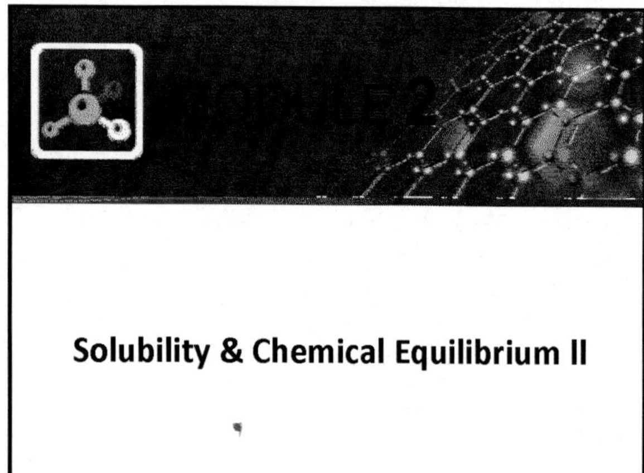
Solubility & Chemical Equilibrium II

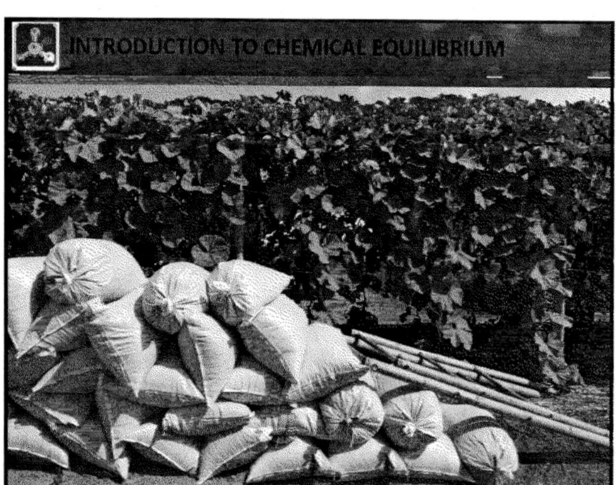
INTRODUCTION TO CHEMICAL EQUILIBRIUM

REACTION QUOTIENT, *Q*

- Chemical processes are reversible
- *Q* is a ratio of activities, *a* at any given time
- *Q* depends on the balanced chemical equation

General Reaction in Aqueous Solution:

$$mA\ (aq) + nB\ (aq) \overset{Q}{\rightleftharpoons} xC\ (aq) + yD\ (aq)$$

$$Q = \frac{a_C^{\,x}\, a_D^{\,y}}{a_A^{\,m}\, a_B^{\,n}}$$

ACTIVITY

- For a **solute**, S:

  $a = \gamma\,[S] / [S]_o$ we use a = [S] (no units)

  where $[S]_o = 1$ mol L^{-1} is the reference state

  γ is the activity coefficient; assume $\gamma = 1$

- For a **gas**, G:

  $a = \gamma\,P_G / P_o$ we use $a = P_G$ (no units)

  where $P_o = 1$ bar is the reference state

  assume $\gamma = 1$

- The activity (a) of a **pure solid or liquid** is 1

  This means we can ignore pure solids or liquids when setting up the equilibrium constant

ACTIVITY & EQUILIBRIUM CONCENTRATIONS

Example: Dissolution of $CaCO_3$(s)

Pure solid → $CaCO_3\,(s) \rightleftharpoons CO_3^{2-}(aq) + Ca^{2+}(aq)$

↑ $a = 1$ (for $CaCO_3$)

$Q = [CO_3^{2-}]\,[Ca^{2+}]$ ⟵ Concentrations at a given time

Q appears unitless because all pressures and concentrations are relative to reference values.

EQUILIBRIUM CONSTANT, *K*

General Reaction in Aqueous Solution:

$$mA\,(aq) + nB\,(aq) \overset{K}{\rightleftharpoons} xC\,(aq) + yD\,(aq)$$

$$K = \frac{a_C^{\,x}\,a_D^{\,y}}{a_A^{\,m}\,a_B^{\,n}}$$

K is dependent on *T*, *P*, pH etc.

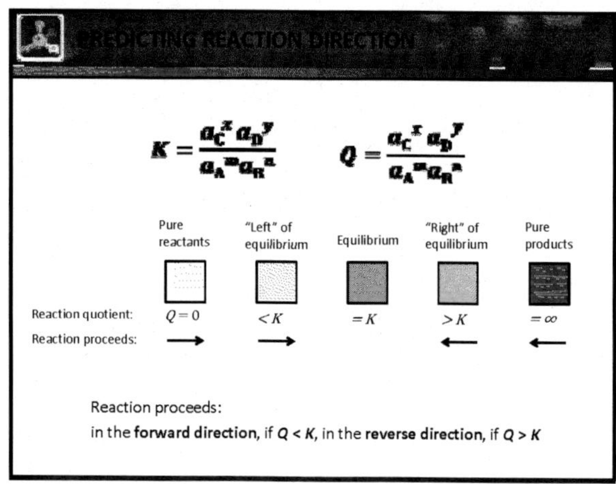

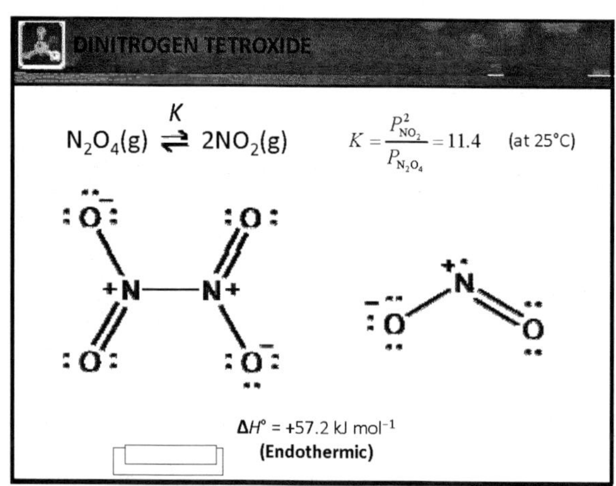

RELATING Q TO K MATHEMATICALLY

1.) Is a mixture of 0.0205 moles NO_2 & 0.750 mol N_2O_4 in a 5.25 L flask at 25°C at equilibrium? If not, in what direction does the reaction shift?

$$Q = \frac{(P_{NO_2})^2}{P_{N_2O_4}} = \frac{(0.0205 \times 0.08314 \times 298.15/5.25)^2}{0.750 \times 0.08314 \times 298.15/5.25} = 0.0137 < K$$

Reaction will proceed in the forward direction – i.e., more NO_2 will be formed until equilibrium is re-established ($Q = K$).

2.) What is K for the reverse reaction associated with dimerization of NO_2?

$$2NO_2(g) \rightleftharpoons N_2O_4(g)$$

$$K_{reverse} = P_{N_2O_4} / (P_{NO_2})^2 = 1/K_{forward} = 1/11.4 = 0.0877$$

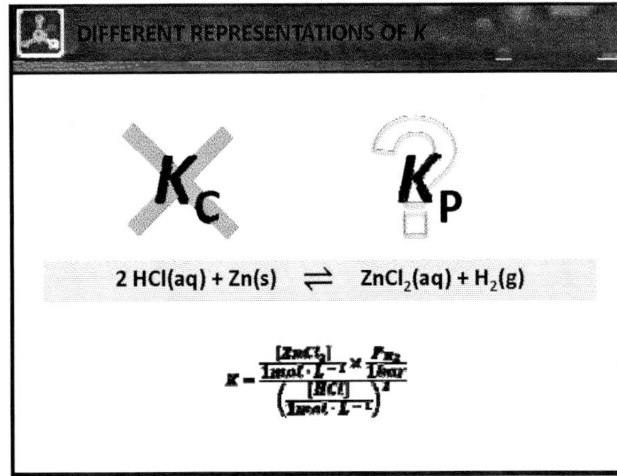

DIFFERENT REPRESENTATIONS OF *K*

- K_a = acid dissociation constant
- K_b = base dissociation constant
- K_w = water autoionization constant
- K_{sp} = solubility product
- K_{ow} = octanol/water partition coefficient

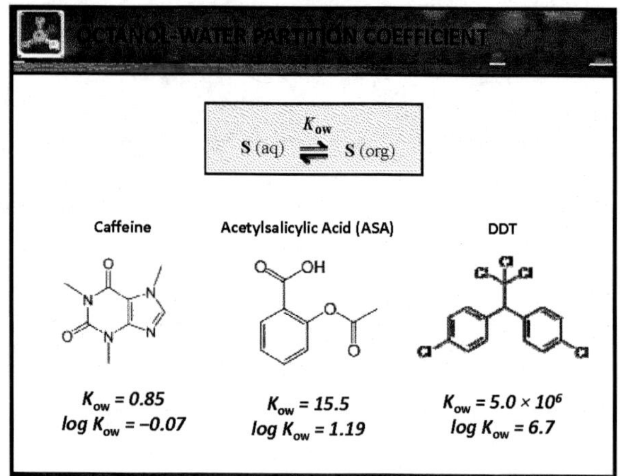

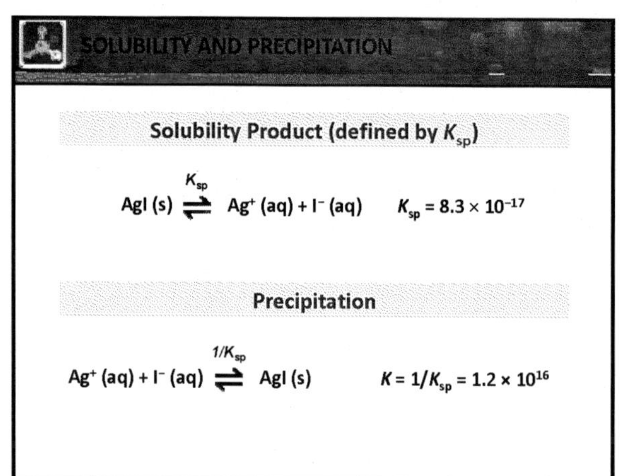

SOLUBILITY PRODUCT FOR SALTS: K_{sp}

Hydroxyapatite

$$Ca_5(PO_4)_3OH\ (s) \overset{K_{sp}}{\rightleftharpoons} 5Ca^{2+}\ (aq) + 3PO_4^{3-}\ (aq) + OH^-\ (aq)$$

$$K_{sp} = [Ca^{2+}]^5\,[PO_4^{3-}]^3\,[OH^-] = 1.0 \times 10^{-36}$$

Fluorapatite

$$Ca_5(PO_4)_3F\ (s) \overset{K_{sp}}{\rightleftharpoons} 5Ca^{2+}\ (aq) + 3PO_4^{3-}\ (aq) + F^-\ (aq)$$

$$K_{sp} = [Ca^{2+}]^5\,[PO_4^{3-}]^3\,[F^-] = 1.0 \times 10^{-60}$$

DIFFERENTIAL SOLUBILITY OF SALTS

Hydroxyapatite:

$$Ca_5(PO_4)_3OH\,(s) \overset{K_{sp}}{\rightleftharpoons} 5Ca^{2+}\,(aq) + 3PO_4^{3-}\,(aq) + OH^-\,(aq)$$

$$K_{sp} = [Ca^{2+}]^5\,[PO_4^{3-}]^3\,[OH^-] = 1.0 \times 10^{-36}$$

Let x = the mol of hydroxylapatite dissolved per litre

$$K_{sp} = (5x)^5\,(3x)^3\,(x) = 84375\,x^9$$

$$x = [K_{sp}/84375]^{1/9} = 2.84 \times 10^{-5}\ M$$ ← **Molar solubility of hydroxyapatite**

DIFFERENTIAL SOLUBILITY OF SALTS

Fluorapatite:

$$Ca_5(PO_4)_3OH\,(s) \overset{K_{sp}}{\rightleftharpoons} 5Ca^{2+}\,(aq) + 3PO_4^{3-}\,(aq) + OH^-\,(aq)$$

$$K_{sp} = [Ca^{2+}]^5\,[PO_4^{3-}]^3\,[F^-] = 1.0 \times 10^{-60}$$

Let x = the mol of fluorapatite dissolved per litre

$$K_{sp} = (5x)^5\,(3x)^3\,(x) = 84375\,x^9$$

$$x = [K_{sp}/84375]^{1/9} = 6.11 \times 10^{-8}\ M$$

$$\frac{2.84 \times 10^{-5}\ M}{6.11 \times 10^{-8}\ M} = \mathbf{460}$$ ← Hydroxyapatite 460-fold <u>more</u> soluble than fluorapatite

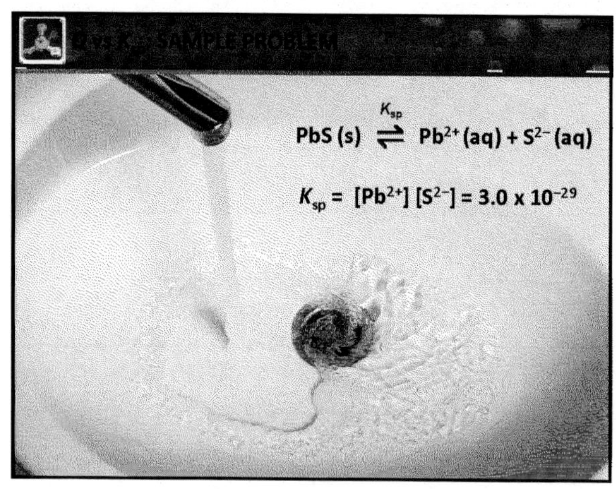

Q vs K_{sp}: SAMPLE PROBLEM

Will a precipitate form if 0.50 mL of 10 μM of K_2S is mixed with 250 mL of 0.10 μM $Pb(NO_3)_2$?

Step 1: $K_2S\ (aq) + Pb(NO_3)_2\ (aq) \xrightleftharpoons{K_{sp}} 2KNO_3\ (aq) + PbS\ (s)$

$PbS\ (s) \xrightleftharpoons{K_{sp}} Pb^{2+}\ (aq) + S^{2-}(aq)$

$K_{sp} = [Pb^{2+}]\ [S^{2-}] = 3.0 \times 10^{-29}$

Step 2:

[Initial] of S^{2-}
After Mixing Solutions:

$$= \frac{(1 \times 10^{-5}\ mol\ L^{-1})(5 \times 10^{-4}\ L)}{2.505 \times 10^{-1}\ L}$$

$= 1.996 \times 10^{-8}\ M$

[Initial] of $Pb(NO_3)_2$
After Mixing Solutions:

$$= \frac{(1 \times 10^{-7}\ mol\ L^{-1})(2.50 \times 10^{-1}\ L)}{2.505 \times 10^{-1}\ L}$$

$= 9.980 \times 10^{-8}\ M$

Step 3: $Q = [Pb^{2+}][S^{2-}] = (9.98 \times 10^{-8})(1.996 \times 10^{-8}) = 2.0 \times 10^{-15} >> K_{sp}$

Therefore, precipitate of PbS (s) will form!

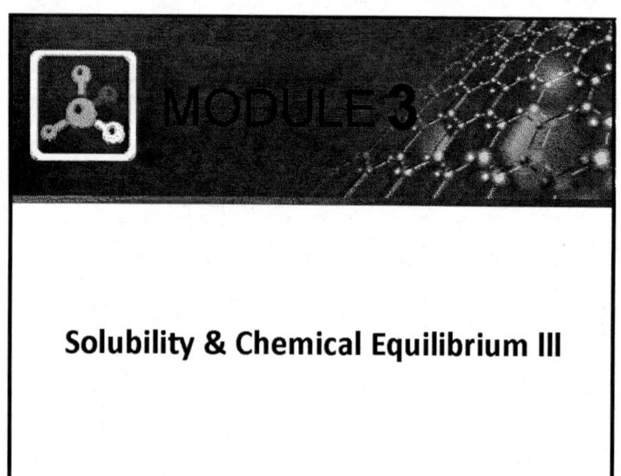

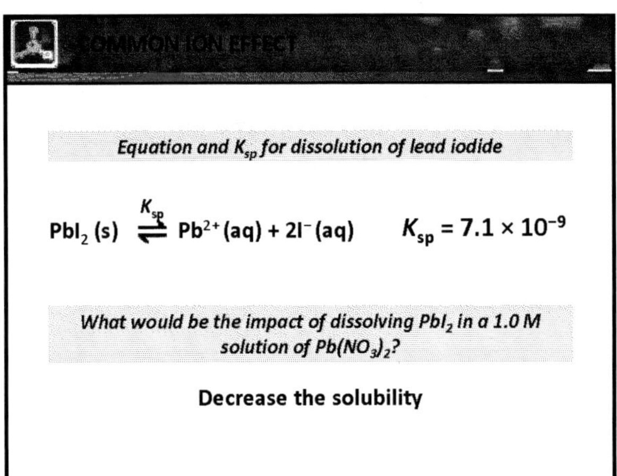

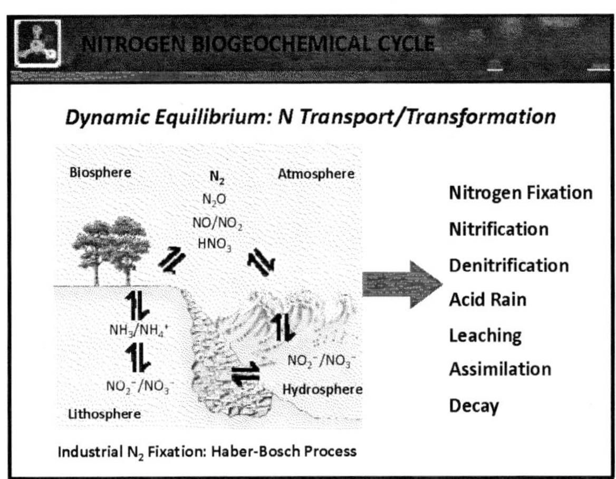

HABER-BOSCH PROCESS

$K = 4.3 \times 10^{-3}$ at 573K

$$N_2\ (g) + 3H_2\ (g) \overset{K}{\rightleftharpoons} 2NH_3\ (g) \quad \Delta H^\circ = -46.1\ \text{kJ mol}^{-1}$$

Feedstocks

$N_2 \rightarrow$ Cyrogenic distillation of air (78% of air, b.p.= −196 °C)

$H_2 \rightarrow$ No natural source; Steam reforming of methane

$$CH_4\ (g) + H_2O\ (g) \rightleftharpoons CO\ (g) + 3H_2\ (g)$$

LE CHATELIER'S PRINCIPLE

Haber-Bosch Process

K = 4.3 × 10^{-3} at 573K
Exothermic Reaction

$$N_2\,(g) + 3H_2\,(g) \overset{K}{\rightleftharpoons} 2NH_3\,(g) \qquad \Delta H^\circ = -46.1 \text{ kJ mol}^{-1}$$

Effect on yield of NH_3?

1. Increase pressure of N_2 → Increase!
2. Decrease pressure of NH_3 → Increase!
3. Increase Temperature → Decrease!
4. Increase all pressures → Increase!

$$Q = \frac{(P_{NH_3})^2}{(P_{N_2})(P_{H_2})^3}$$

Would the addition of an inert gas or **catalyst** impact the yield? **NO**

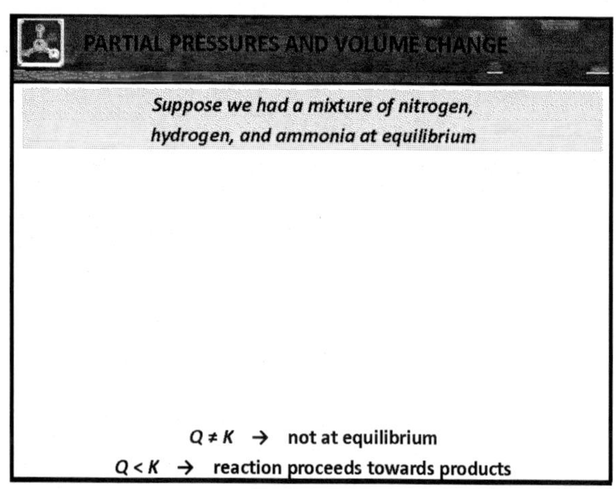

PARTIAL PRESSURES AND VOLUME CHANGE
Suppose we had a mixture of nitrogen, hydrogen, and ammonia at equilibrium
Q ≠ K → not at equilibrium
Q < K → reaction proceeds towards products

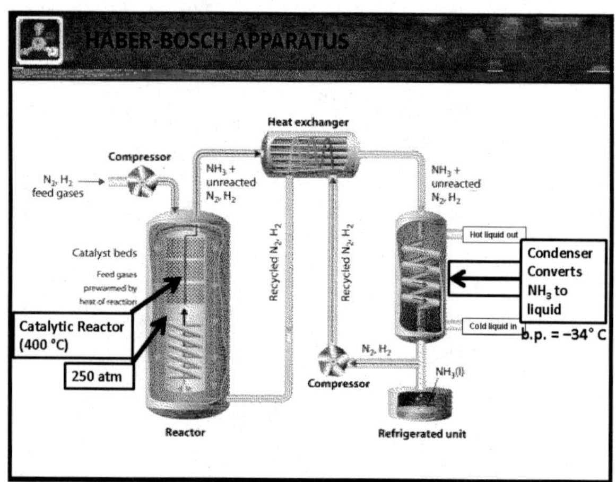

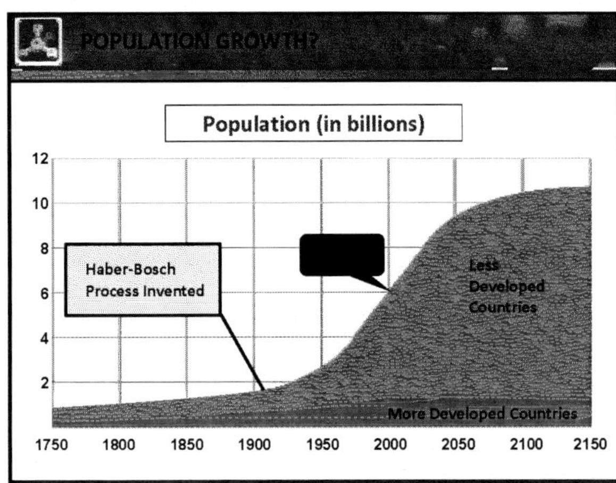
POPULATION GROWTH?
Population (in billions)
12
10
8
6
4
2
1750
1800
1850
1900
1950
2000
2050
2100
2150
Haber-Bosch Process Invented
Less Developed Countries
More Developed Countries

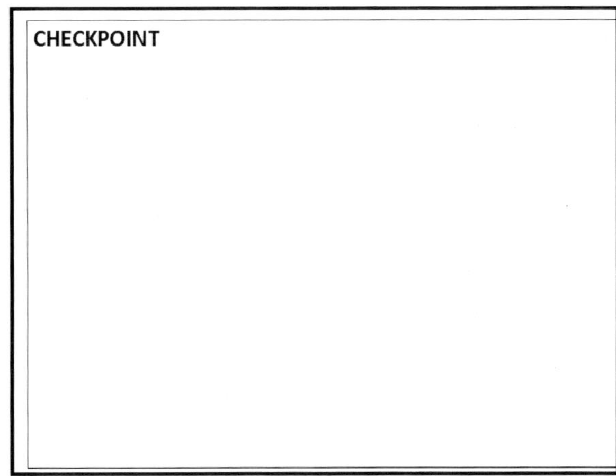
CHECKPOINT

AMMONIUM NITRATE
NH3(g) + HNO3(aq) ⟶ NH4NO3(aq) ⟶ NH4NO3(s)
Explosives!

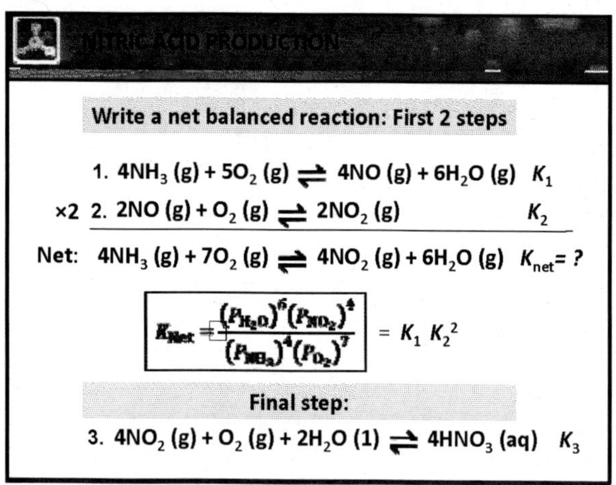

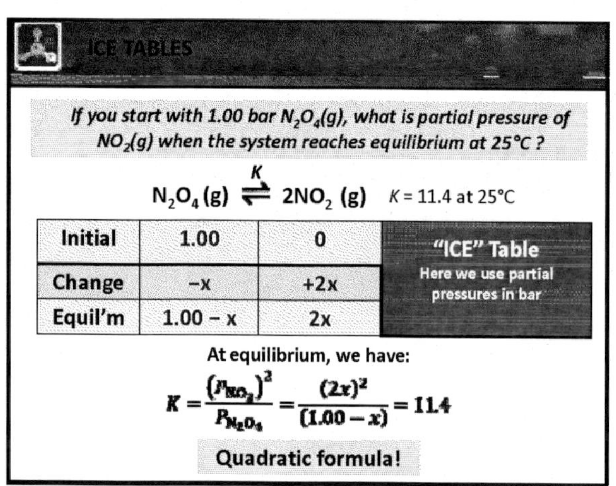

NITRIC ACID PRODUCTION
Write a net balanced reaction: First 2 steps

$K_{Net} = \frac{(P_{H_2O})^6 (P_{NO_2})^4}{(P_{NH_3})^4 (P_{O_2})^7} = K_1\,K_2^2$
Final step:

ICE TABLES
If you start with 1.00 bar $N_2O_4(g)$, what is partial pressure of $NO_2(g)$ when the system reaches equilibrium at 25°C ?
$N_2O_4\,(g) \overset{K}{\rightleftharpoons} 2NO_2\,(g)$ $K = 11.4$ at 25°C
Initial | 1.00 | 0
Change | −x | +2x
Equil'm | 1.00 − x | 2x
"ICE" Table
Here we use partial pressures in bar
At equilibrium, we have:
$K = \frac{(P_{NO_2})^2}{P_{N_2O_4}} = \frac{(2x)^2}{(1.00 - x)} = 11.4$
Quadratic formula!

QUADRATIC FORMULA

Solving for *x*:

$$4x^2 = 11.4(1-x)$$

Rearranged into standard quadratic form, gives:

$$4x^2 + 11.4x - 11.4 = 0$$

Quadratic formula:

$$x = \frac{-b \pm \sqrt{b^2 - 4ac}}{2a}$$

$x = 0.7842$ bar ***or*** $x = -3.634$ bar
(but negative P makes no sense)

Therefore $P_{NO_2} = 2x = 1.568$ bar at equilibrium

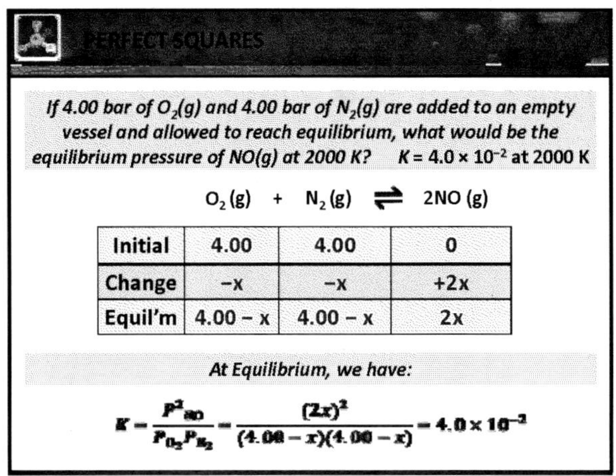

PERFECT SQUARES
If 4.00 bar of $O_2(g)$ and 4.00 bar of $N_2(g)$ are added to an empty vessel and allowed to reach equilibrium, what would be the equilibrium pressure of NO(g) at 2000 K? $K = 4.0 \times 10^{-2}$ at 2000 K
O_2 (g) + N_2 (g) ⇌ 2NO (g)
Initial | 4.00 | 4.00 | 0
Change | −x | −x | +2x
Equil'm | 4.00 − x | 4.00 − x | 2x
At Equilibrium, we have:
$K = \frac{P^2_{NO}}{P_{O_2}P_{N_2}} = \frac{(2x)^2}{(4.00 - x)(4.00 - x)} = 4.0 \times 10^{-2}$

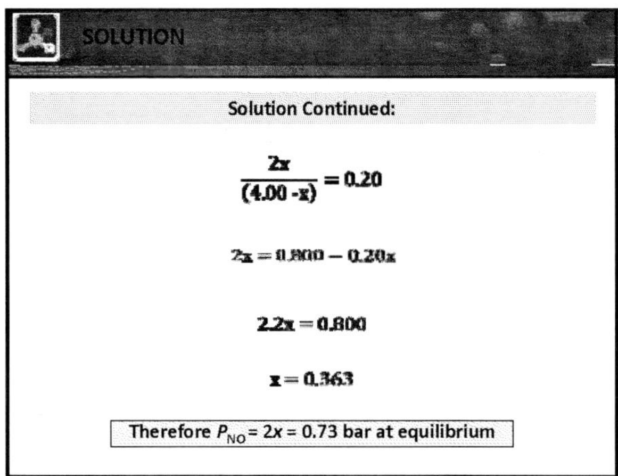

SOLUTION
Solution Continued:
$\frac{2x}{(4.00 - x)} = 0.20$
$2x = 0.800 - 0.20x$
$2.2x = 0.800$
$x = 0.363$
Therefore $P_{NO} = 2x = 0.73$ bar at equilibrium

OBJECTIVES

1. Identify the unique properties of water and the characteristics that lead to these properties
2. Define strong, weak and non-electrolytes
3. Apply the rules for solubility to predict formation of precipitates, and calculate molar solubility
4. Define *Q* and *K* using activities
5. Predict the direction in which an equilibrium proceeds
6. State and apply Le Châtelier's principle
7. Solve quantitative equilibrium problems, including with the use of an "ICE" table

Unit 6

Most important concepts:

-
-
-
-
-
-
-
-
-
-
-
-

Unit 6

Questions I have:

-
-
-
-
-
-
-
-
-
-
-
-

UNIT 7 - Acid-Base Chemistry

INTRODUCTION

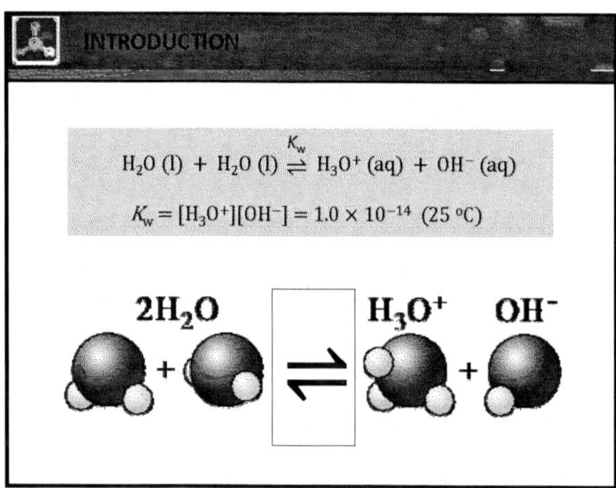

MODULE 1

Acid-Base Chemistry I

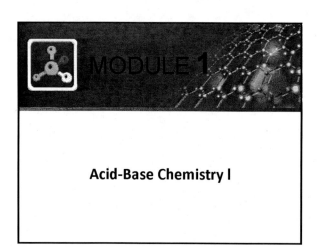

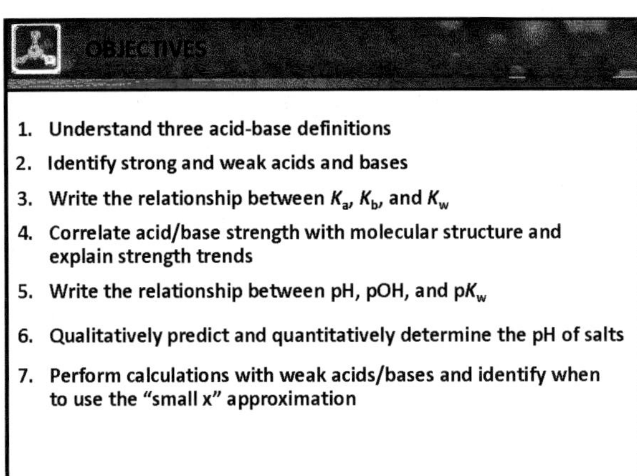
OBJECTIVES
1. Understand three acid-base definitions
2. Identify strong and weak acids and bases
3. Write the relationship between K_a, K_b, and K_w
4. Correlate acid/base strength with molecular structure and explain strength trends
5. Write the relationship between pH, pOH, and pK_w
6. Qualitatively predict and quantitatively determine the pH of salts
7. Perform calculations with weak acids/bases and identify when to use the "small x" approximation

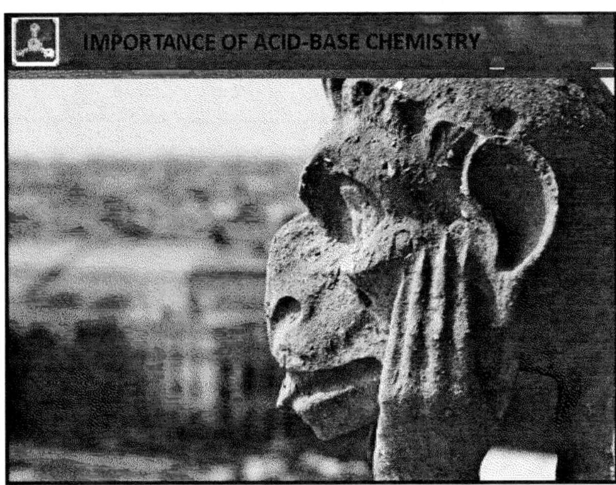
IMPORTANCE OF ACID-BASE CHEMISTRY

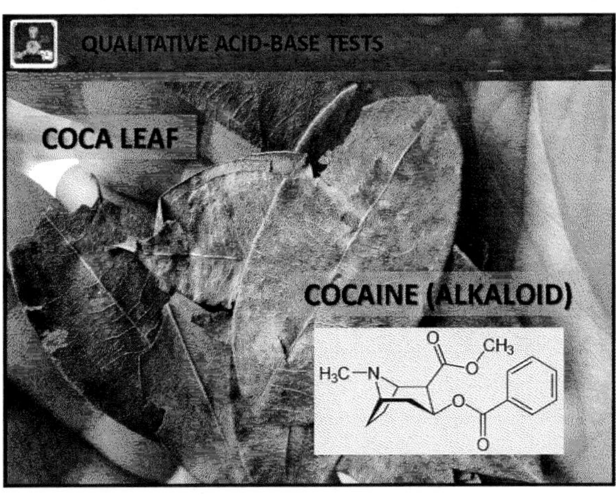
QUALITATIVE ACID-BASE TESTS
COCA LEAF
COCAINE (ALKALOID)
O
CH3
H3C—N
O
O
O

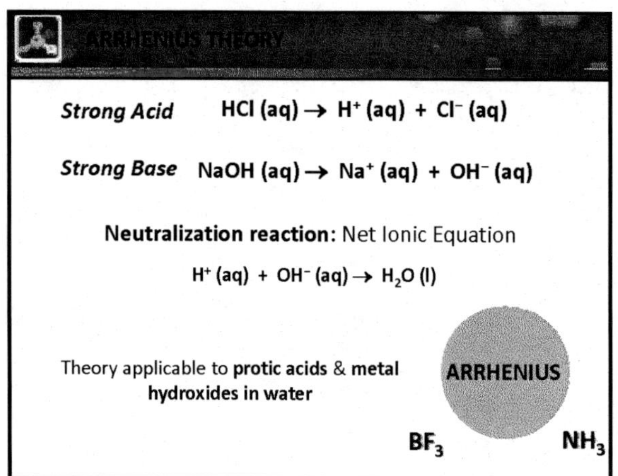

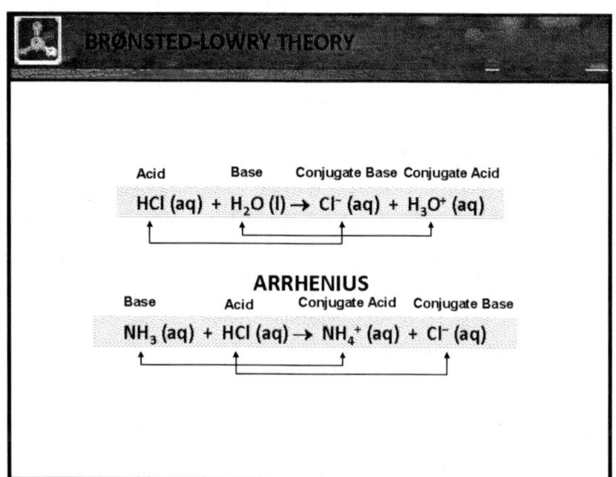

RELATIVE STRENGTH OF ACID-BASE CONJUGATES

$HCl + OH^- \longrightarrow Cl^- + H_2O$

$H_2O + I^- \longleftarrow OH^- + HI$

Increasing acid strength ↑ | Increasing base strength ↓

Acid		Conjugate base	
Perchloric acid	$HClO_4$	Perchlorate ion	ClO_4^-
★ Hydroiodic acid	HI	★ Iodide ion	I^-
Hydrobromic acid	HBr	Bromide ion	Br^-
★ Hydrochloric acid	HCl	★ Chloride ion	Cl^-
Sulfuric acid	H_2SO_4	Hydrogen sulfate ion	HSO_4^-
Nitric acid	HNO_3	Nitrate ion	NO_3^-
Hydronium ion*	H_3O^+	Water*	H_2O
Hydrogen sulfate ion	HSO_4^-	Sulfate ion	SO_4^{2-}
Nitrous acid	HNO_2	Nitrite ion	NO_2^-
Acetic acid	$HC_2H_3O_2$	Acetate ion	$C_2H_3O_2^-$
Carbonic acid	H_2CO_3	Hydrogen carbonate ion	HCO_3^-
Ammonium ion	NH_4^+	Ammonia	NH_3
Hydrogen carbonate ion	HCO_3^-	Carbonate ion	CO_3^{2-}
★ Water	H_2O	★ Hydroxide ion	OH^-
Methanol	CH_3OH	Methoxide ion	CH_3O^-
Ammonia	NH_3	Amide ion	NH_2^-

Stronger the acid (or base) ⟶ Weaker its conjugate base (or acid)

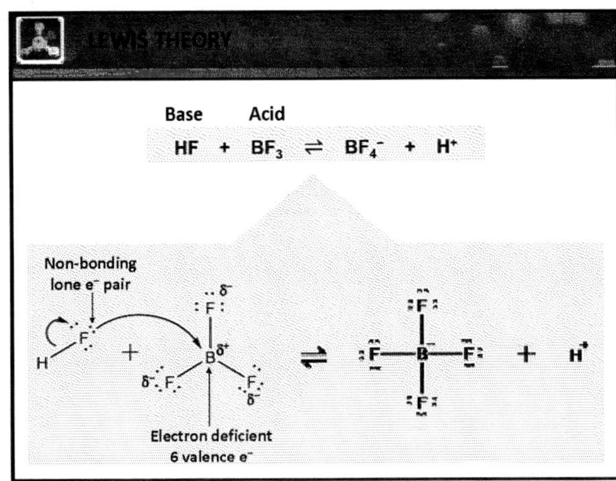
LEWIS THEORY
Base
Acid
HF + BF3 ⇌ BF4- + H+
Non-bonding
lone e- pair
Electron deficient
6 valence e-

CHECKPOINT

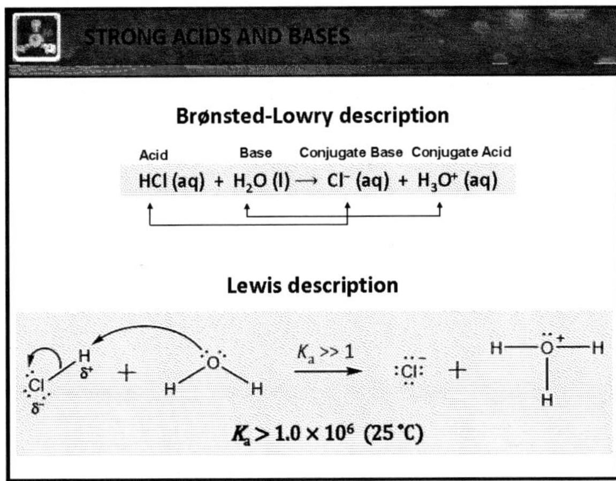
STRONG ACIDS AND BASES
Brønsted-Lowry description
Acid
Base
Conjugate Base
Conjugate Acid
HCl (aq) + H2O (l) → Cl- (aq) + H3O+ (aq)
Lewis description
Ka >> 1
Ka > 1.0 × 10^6 (25 °C)

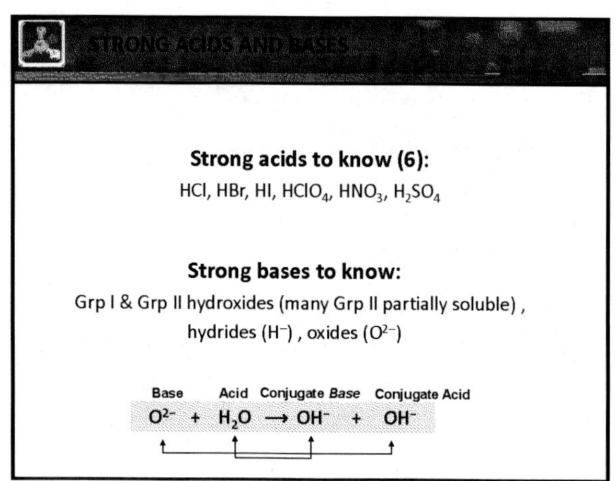

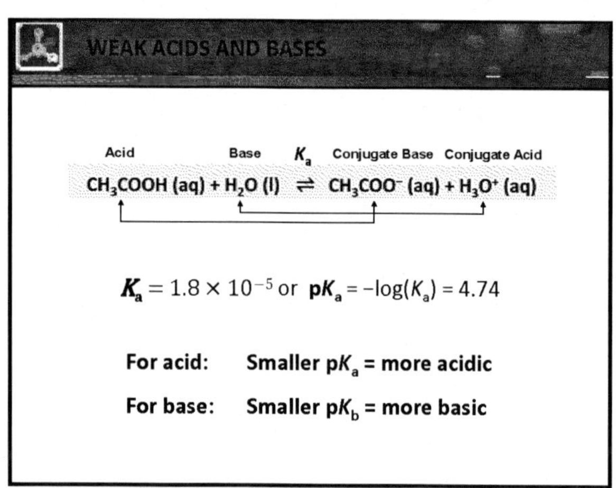

WEAK ACIDS AND BASES

WEAK BASES

NH_3	CH_3NH_2	$(CH_3H_2)_2NH$
ammonia	methylamine	diethylamine
$pK_b = 4.74$	$pK_b = 3.36$	$pK_b = 3.16$

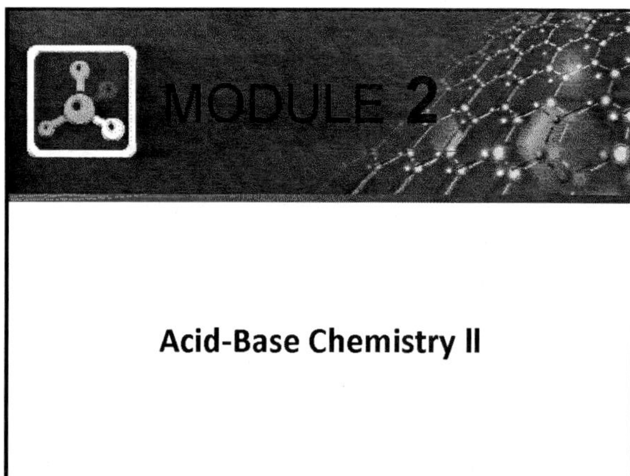

WEAK ACIDS AND K_a

Acid		Base	K_a	Conjugate Base		Conjugate Acid
CH_3COOH (aq)	+	H_2O (l)	$\rightleftharpoons$	CH_3COO^- (aq)	+	H_3O^+ (aq)

$$K_a = \frac{[CH_3COO^-][H_3O^+]}{[CH_3COOH]} = 1.8 \times 10^{-5}$$

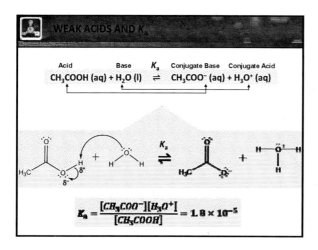

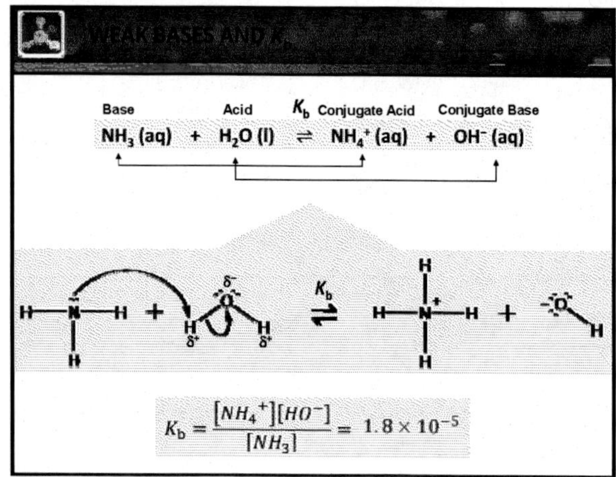
WEAK BASES AND K_b
Base Acid K_b Conjugate Acid Conjugate Base
NH_3 (aq) + H_2O (l) ⇌ NH_4^+ (aq) + OH^- (aq)
K_b
$K_b = \frac{[NH_4^+][HO^-]}{[NH_3]} = 1.8 \times 10^{-5}$

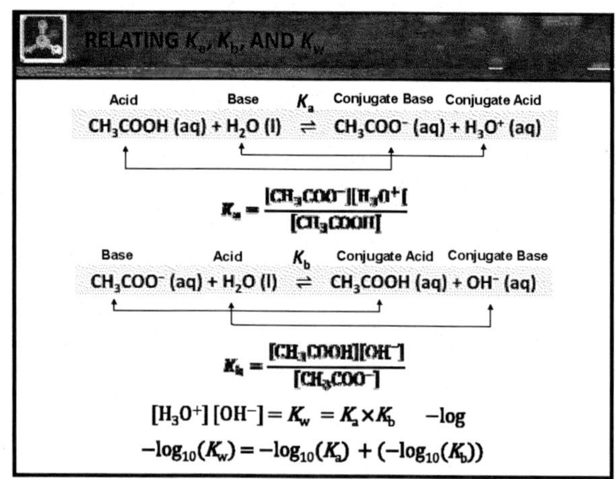
RELATING K_a, K_b, AND K_w
Acid Base K_a Conjugate Base Conjugate Acid
CH_3COOH (aq) + H_2O (l) ⇌ CH_3COO^- (aq) + H_3O^+ (aq)
$K_a = \frac{[CH_3COO^-][H_3O^+]}{[CH_3COOH]}$
Base Acid K_b Conjugate Acid Conjugate Base
CH_3COO^- (aq) + H_2O (l) ⇌ CH_3COOH (aq) + OH^- (aq)
$K_b = \frac{[CH_3COOH][OH^-]}{[CH_3COO^-]}$
$[H_3O^+][OH^-] = K_w = K_a \times K_b$ −log
$-\log_{10}(K_w) = -\log_{10}(K_a) + (-\log_{10}(K_b))$

pK_A & pK_B RELATIONSHIP

$pK_w = pK_a + pK_b = 14.000$ — For a conjugate acid-base pair

NH_3 as Weak Base *vs.* NH_4^+ as Weak Acid

1. $K_b = 1.8 \times 10^{-5}$ ⇨ 2. $pK_b = 4.74$ ⇨ 3. $pK_a = 14.0 - 4.74 = 9.26$
4. $K_a = 10^{-9.26} = 5.5 \times 10^{-10}$

CH_3COOH as Weak Acid *vs.* CH_3COO^- as Weak Base

1. $K_a = 1.8 \times 10^{-5}$ ⇨ 2. $pK_a = 4.74$ ⇨ 3. $pK_b = 14.0 - 4.74 = 9.26$
4. $K_b = 10^{-9.26} = 5.5 \times 10^{-10}$

CH_3COOH & NH_4^+ are both weak acids ($K_a < 1$)
NH_3 & CH_3COO^- are both weak bases ($K_b < 1$)

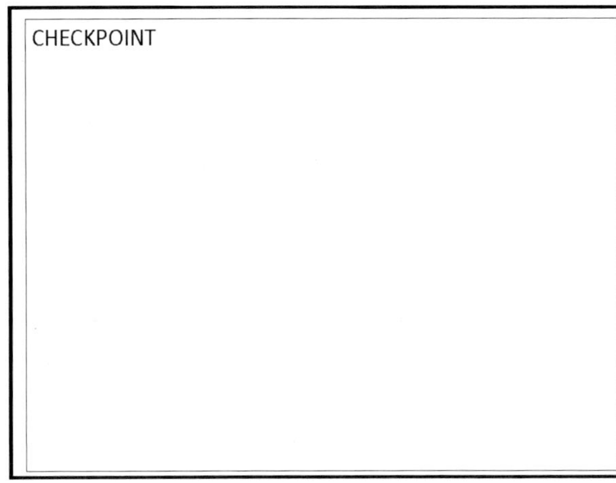
CHECKPOINT

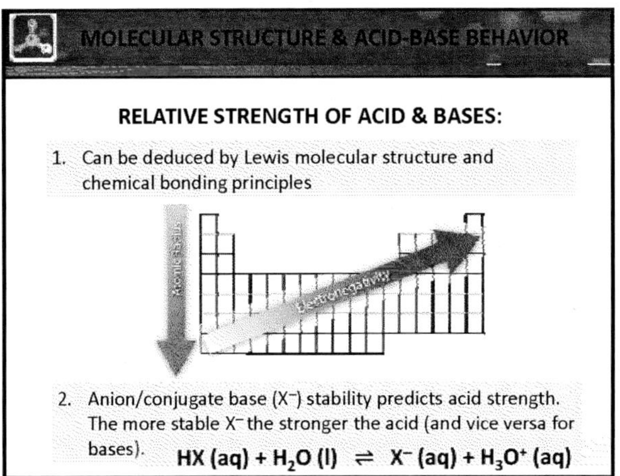
MOLECULAR STRUCTURE & ACID-BASE BEHAVIOR
RELATIVE STRENGTH OF ACID & BASES:
1. Can be deduced by Lewis molecular structure and chemical bonding principles
Atomic Radius
Electronegativity
2. Anion/conjugate base (X⁻) stability predicts acid strength. The more stable X⁻ the stronger the acid (and vice versa for bases).
HX (aq) + H2O (l) ⇌ X⁻ (aq) + H3O⁺ (aq)

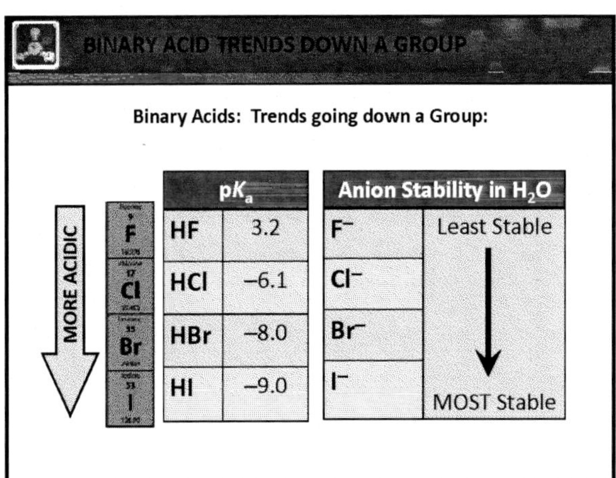
BINARY ACID TRENDS DOWN A GROUP
Binary Acids: Trends going down a Group:
MORE ACIDIC
F
Cl
Br
I
pKa
HF 3.2
HCl −6.1
HBr −8.0
HI −9.0
Anion Stability in H2O
F⁻
Cl⁻
Br⁻
I⁻
Least Stable
MOST Stable

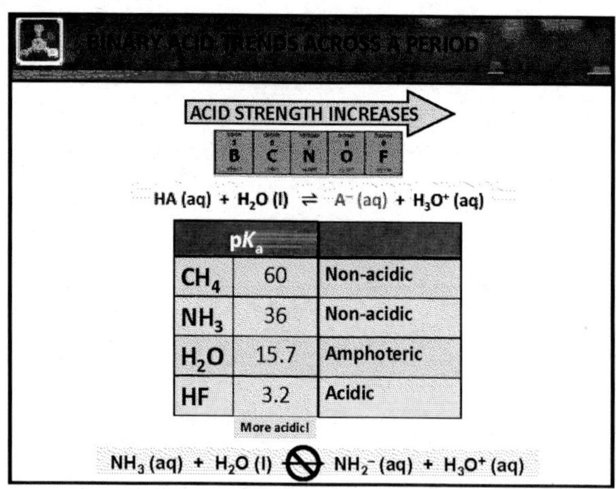

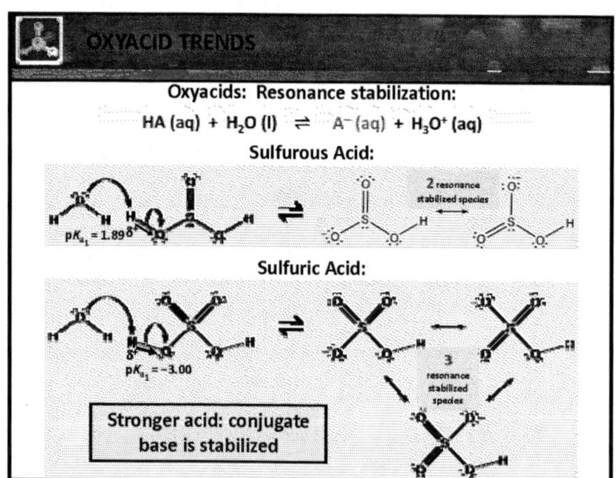

OXYACID TRENDS

For systems with same number of O atoms, the electronegativity of the central atom differentiates strength (negative charge is always on oxygen):

H-O-Cl	H-O-Br
$K_a = 2.9 \times 10^{-8}$	$K_a = 2.1 \times 10^{-9}$
EN (Cl) = 3.0	EN (Br) = 2.8

H — O — Cl

CHECKPOINT

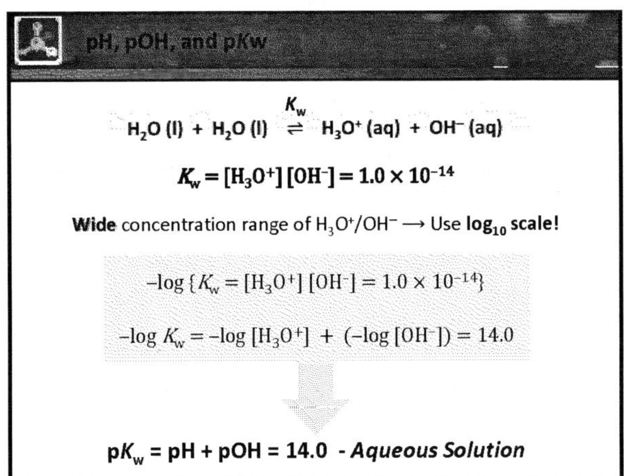
pH, pOH, and pKw
$H_2O\ (l) + H_2O\ (l) \overset{K_w}{\rightleftharpoons} H_3O^+\ (aq) + OH^-\ (aq)$
$K_w = [H_3O^+][OH^-] = 1.0 \times 10^{-14}$
Wide concentration range of H_3O^+/OH^- ⟶ Use $\log_{10}$ scale!
$-\log\ \{K_w = [H_3O^+][OH^-] = 1.0 \times 10^{-14}\}$
$-\log K_w = -\log [H_3O^+] + (-\log [OH^-]) = 14.0$
$pK_w = pH + pOH = 14.0$ - *Aqueous Solution*

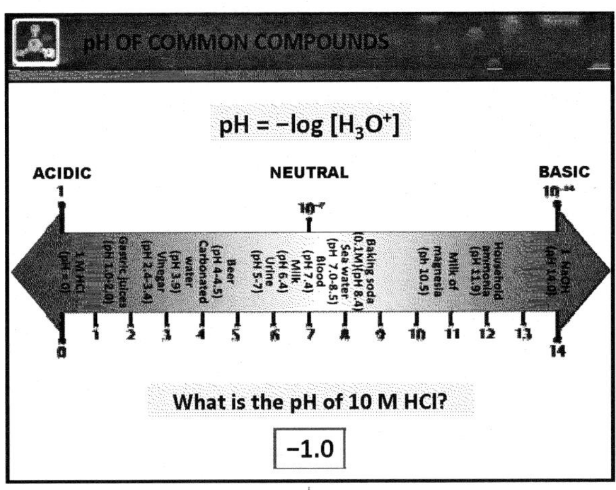
pH OF COMMON COMPOUNDS
$pH = -\log [H_3O^+]$
ACIDIC
1
NEUTRAL
10^{-7}
BASIC
1 M HCl (pH = 0)
Gastric juices (pH 1.0-2.0)
Vinegar (pH 2.4-3.4)
(pH 3.9) Carbonated water
Beer (pH 4-4.5)
Urine (pH 5-7)
Milk (pH 6.4)
Blood (pH 7.4)
Sea water (pH 7.0-8.5)
Baking soda (0.1M)(pH 8.4)
Milk of magnesia (ph 10.5)
Household ammonia (pH 11.9)
1 NaOH (pH 14.0)
0 1 2 3 4 5 6 7 8 9 10 11 12 13 14
What is the pH of 10 M HCl?
−1.0

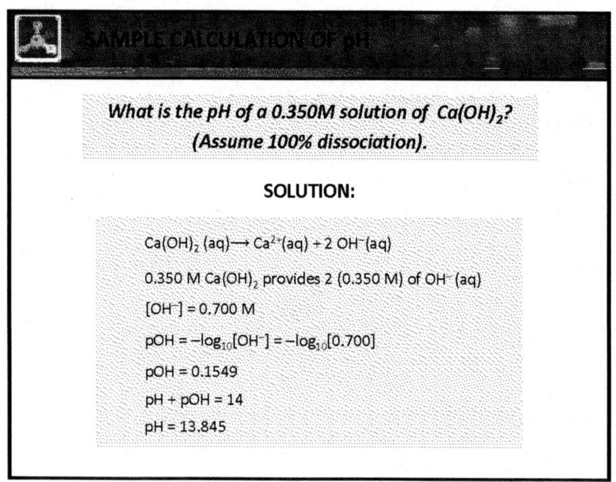
SAMPLE CALCULATION OF pH
What is the pH of a 0.350M solution of $Ca(OH)_2$?
(Assume 100% dissociation).
SOLUTION:
$Ca(OH)_2$ (aq) ⟶ Ca^{2+}(aq) + 2 OH^-(aq)
0.350 M $Ca(OH)_2$ provides 2 (0.350 M) of OH^- (aq)
$[OH^-] = 0.700$ M
$pOH = -\log_{10}[OH^-] = -\log_{10}[0.700]$
pOH = 0.1549
pH + pOH = 14
pH = 13.845

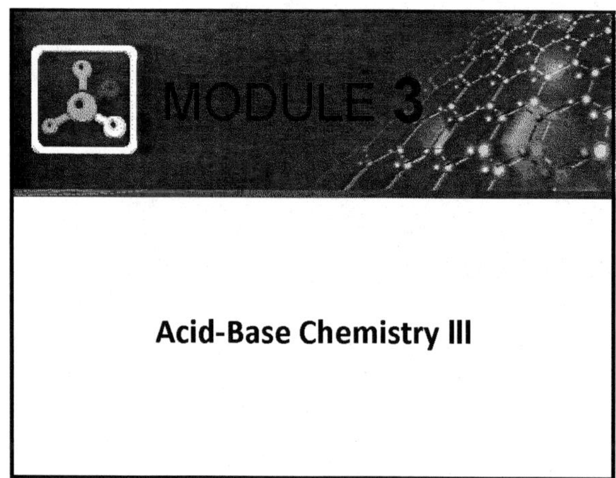
MODULE 3
Acid-Base Chemistry III

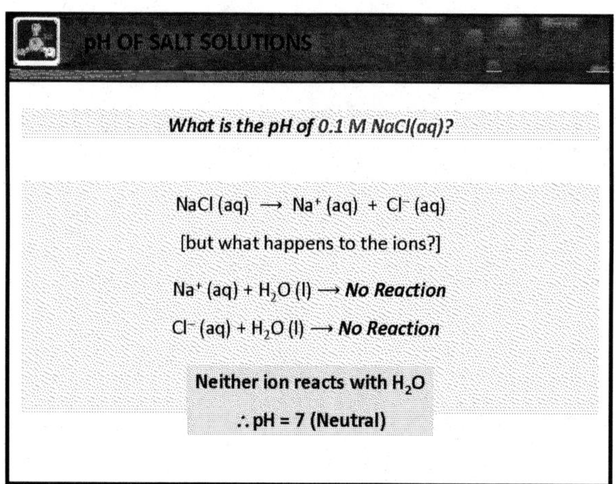
pH OF SALT SOLUTIONS
What is the pH of 0.1 M NaCl(aq)?
NaCl (aq) ⟶ Na^+ (aq) + Cl^- (aq)
[but what happens to the ions?]
Na^+ (aq) + H_2O (l) ⟶ No Reaction
Cl^- (aq) + H_2O (l) ⟶ No Reaction
Neither ion reacts with H_2O
∴ pH = 7 (Neutral)

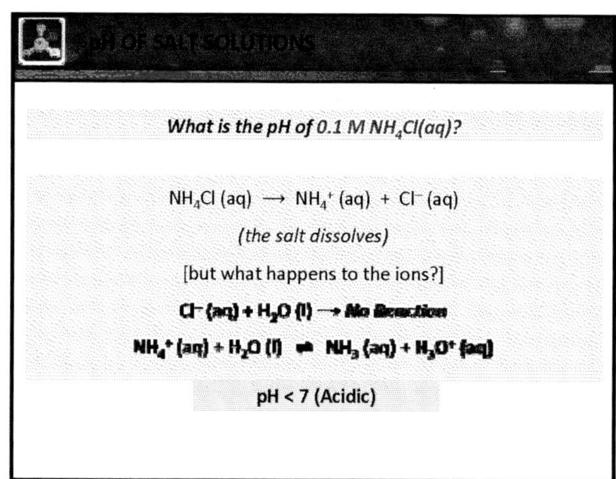
pH OF SALT SOLUTIONS
What is the pH of 0.1 M NH4Cl(aq)?
NH4Cl (aq) → NH4+ (aq) + Cl− (aq)
(the salt dissolves)
[but what happens to the ions?]
Cl− (aq) + H2O (l) → No Reaction
NH4+ (aq) + H2O (l) ⇌ NH3 (aq) + H3O+ (aq)
pH < 7 (Acidic)

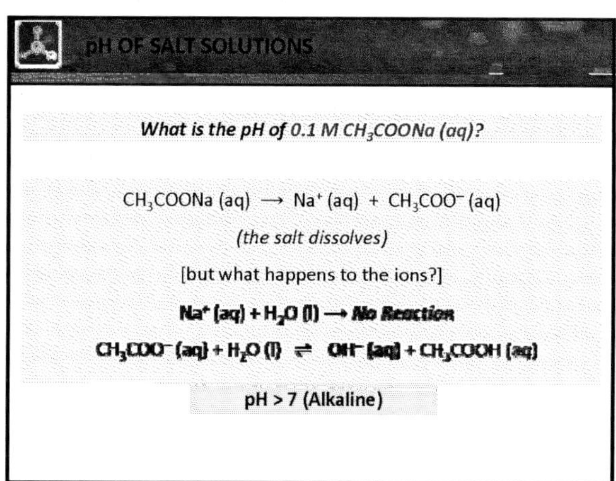
pH OF SALT SOLUTIONS
What is the pH of 0.1 M CH3COONa (aq)?
CH3COONa (aq) → Na+ (aq) + CH3COO− (aq)
(the salt dissolves)
[but what happens to the ions?]
Na+ (aq) + H2O (l) → No Reaction
CH3COO− (aq) + H2O (l) ⇌ OH− (aq) + CH3COOH (aq)
pH > 7 (Alkaline)

pH OF SALT SOLUTIONS

What is the pH of 0.1 M NH_4CH_3COO dissolved in de-ionized water?
K_a (CH_3COOH) = 1.8×10^{-5}, K_b (NH_3) = 1.8×10^{-5}

NH_4CH_3COO (aq) → NH_4^+ (aq) + CH_3COO^- (aq)

and the ions:

$$CH_3COO^- (aq) + H_2O (l) \overset{K_b}{\rightleftharpoons} CH_3COOH (aq) + OH^- (aq)$$

$$NH_4^+ (aq) + H_2O (l) \overset{K_a}{\rightleftharpoons} NH_3 (aq) + H_3O^+ (aq)$$

Acidic or Alkaline Solution?

$K_b = 5.5 \times 10^{-10}$ and $K_a = 5.5 \times 10^{-10}$

pH = 7 (Neutral) because of equal magnitudes of K_a & K_b (larger magnitude K prevails)

CHECKPOINT

WEAK ACIDS & BASES: ICE TABLES

Determine the pH and % ionization of a 0.100 M solution of acetic acid. K_a (CH_3COOH = 1.8 x 10^{-5})

[Write down the chemistry correctly!]

$$CH_3COOH\,(aq) + H_2O\,(l) \overset{K_a}{\rightleftharpoons} CH_3COO^-\,(aq) + H_3O^+\,(aq)$$

	CH_3COOH	H_2O	CH_3COO^-	H_3O^+
Initial	0.100 M		0 M	0 M
Change	−x M		+x M	+x M
Equil'm	0.100 − x M		x M	x M

$$K_a = \frac{[CH_3COO^-][H_3O^+]}{[CH_3COOH]} = \frac{x^2}{0.100 - x} = 1.8 \times 10^{-5}$$

Assume x << 0.100, then (0.100 – x) ≈ 0.100

SMALL x APPROXIMATION

Check: If $\frac{[HA]}{K_a} > 100$ *, then assumption is valid (< 5% error):*

$$\frac{0.100}{1.8 \times 10^{-5}} = 5.6 \times 10^3, \text{ which is} > 100$$

Then: $x^2 = (0.100)(1.8 \times 10^{-5})$; $x = [H_3O^+] = 1.34 \times 10^{-3}$

and: **pH** = $-\log(1.34 \times 10^{-3})$ = **2.87**

% Ionization:

$$\frac{[H_3O^+]}{[HA]_{initial}} \times 100 = \frac{1.3_4 \times 10^{-3}\,M}{0.100\,M} \times 100 = 1.3\%$$

QUADRATIC FORMULA

Determine the pH and % ionization of 0.00050% by mass acetic acid.

Assume 1.0 L ∴ $[1000\ g\ L^{-1} \times (5.0 \times 10^{-4}/100)] / 60.022\ g\ mol^{-1} = 8.33 \times 10^{-5}$

$$CH_3COOH\,(aq) + H_2O\,(l) \overset{K_a}{\rightleftharpoons} CH_3COO^-\,(aq) + H_3O^+\,(aq)$$

Initial	8.33×10^{-5} M			
Change	−x M		+x	+x
Equi'm	8.33×10^{-5} − x M		x	x

$$K_a = \frac{[CH_3COO^-][H_3O^+]}{[CH_3COOH]} = \frac{x^2}{8.33 \times 10^{-5} - x} = 1.8 \times 10^{-5}$$

$$\frac{8.33 \times 10^{-5}}{1.8 \times 10^{-5}} = 4.6$$ < 100

Require use of quadratic equation because of the dilute conc. of weak acid!

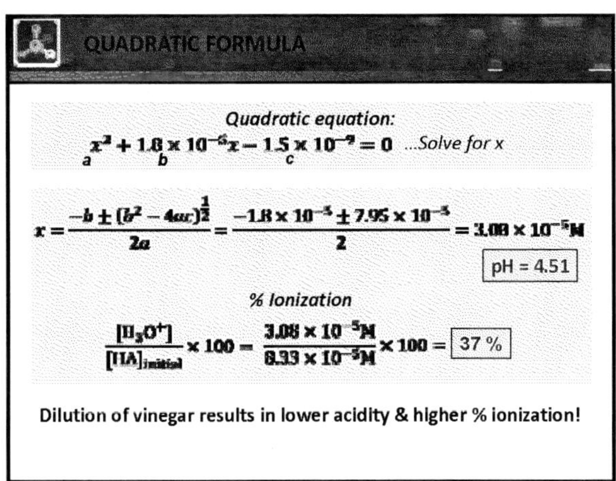

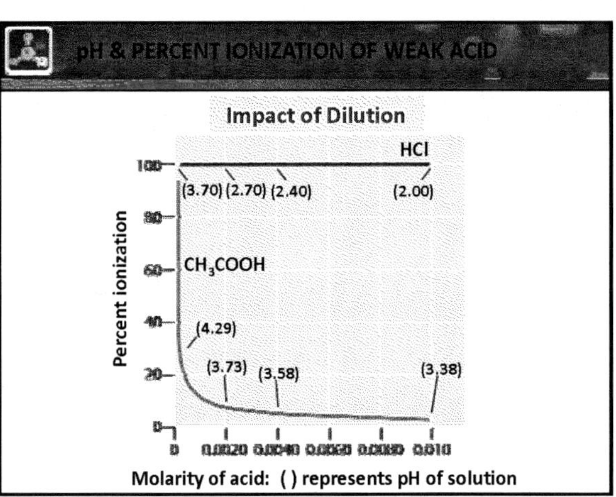

SAMPLE CALCULATION

What is the pH of a 0.350 M solution of NaF? (K_a HF = 6.6 × 10^{-4})

$$F^-(aq) + H_2O(l) \overset{K_b}{\rightleftharpoons} HF(aq) + OH^-(aq)$$

Initial	0.350 M			
Change	−x		+x	+x
Equil'm	0.350 − x M		x	x

$$K_b = \frac{[HF][OH^-]}{[F^-]} = \frac{x^2}{0.350 - x} = \frac{1.0 \times 10^{-14}}{6.6 \times 10^{-4}} = 1.52 \times 10^{-11}$$

Assume x << 0.350, then (0.350 − x) ≈ 0.350

$$\frac{[base]}{K_b} > 100$$ Assumption is valid

Then: $x^2 = (0.350)(1.52 \times 10^{-11})$; $x = [OH^-] = 2.31 \times 10^{-6}$

And: **pOH** = $-\log(2.31 \times 10^{-6}) = 5.636$; **pH = 14.00 − 5.636 = 8.36**

CHECKPOINT

OBJECTIVES

1. **Understand three acid-base definitions**
2. **Identify strong and weak acids and bases**
3. **Write the relationship between K_a, K_b, and K_w**
4. **Correlate acid/base strength with molecular structure and explain strength trends**
5. **Write the relationship between pH, pOH, and pK_w**
6. **Qualitatively predict and quantitatively determine the pH of salts**
7. **Perform calculations with weak acids/bases and identify when to use the "small x" approximation**

Unit 7

Most important concepts:

-
-
-
-
-
-
-
-
-
-
-
-

Unit 7

Questions I have:

-
-
-
-
-
-
-
-
-
-
-
-

UNIT 8 - Thermochemistry

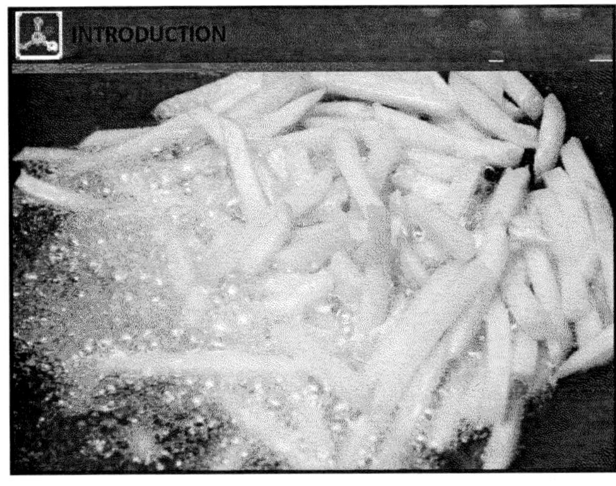

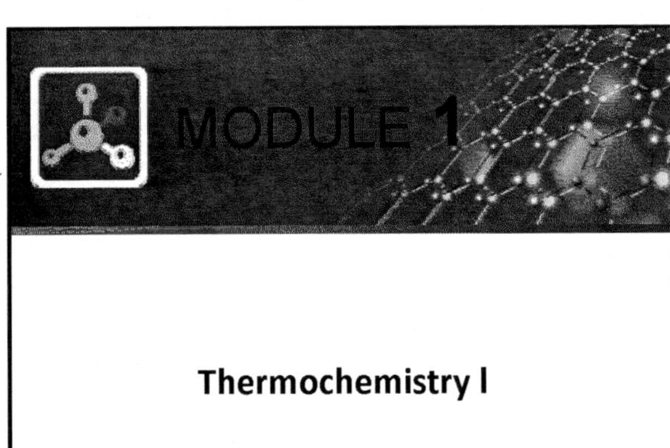

Thermochemistry I

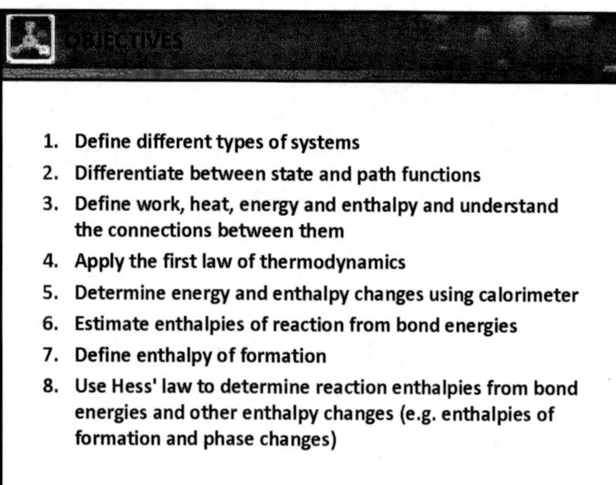
OBJECTIVES
1. Define different types of systems
2. Differentiate between state and path functions
3. Define work, heat, energy and enthalpy and understand the connections between them
4. Apply the first law of thermodynamics
5. Determine energy and enthalpy changes using calorimeter
6. Estimate enthalpies of reaction from bond energies
7. Define enthalpy of formation
8. Use Hess' law to determine reaction enthalpies from bond energies and other enthalpy changes (e.g. enthalpies of formation and phase changes)

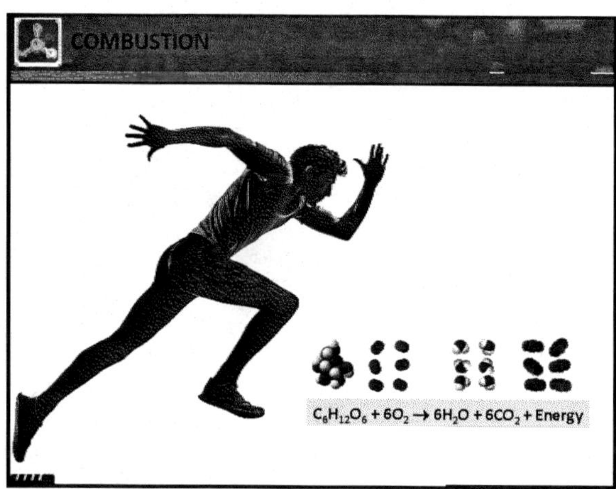
COMBUSTION
$C_6H_{12}O_6 + 6O_2 \rightarrow 6H_2O + 6CO_2 + Energy$

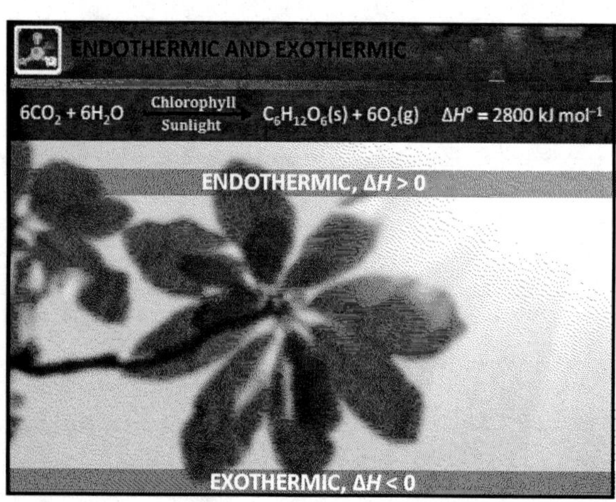
ENDOTHERMIC AND EXOTHERMIC
$6CO_2 + 6H_2O \xrightarrow[\text{Sunlight}]{\text{Chlorophyll}} C_6H_{12}O_6(s) + 6O_2(g) \quad \Delta H° = 2800\ kJ\ mol^{-1}$
ENDOTHERMIC, $\Delta H > 0$
EXOTHERMIC, $\Delta H < 0$

SYSTEM VERSUS SURROUNDINGS

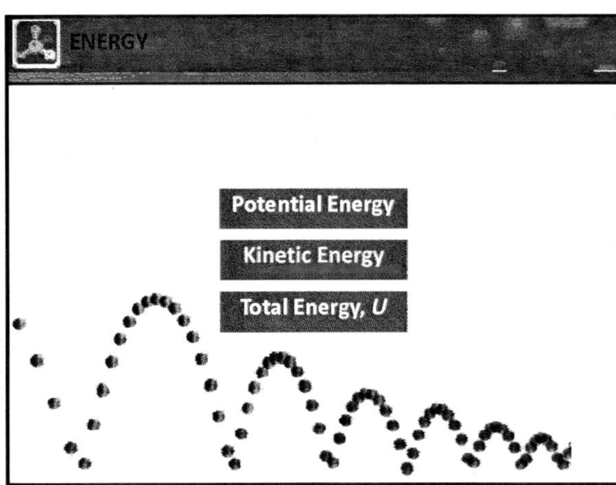
ENERGY
Potential Energy
Kinetic Energy
Total Energy, U

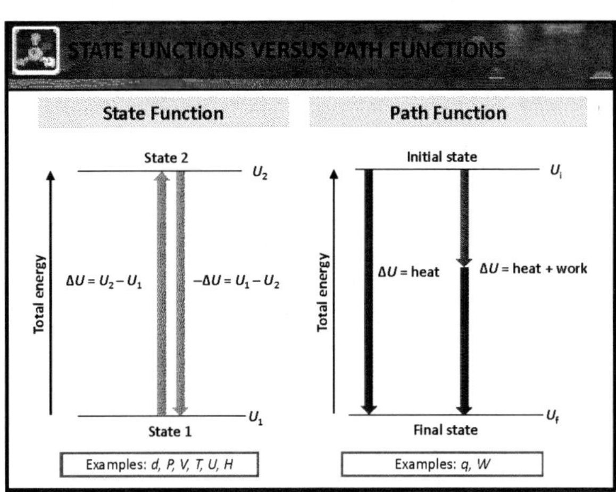
STATE FUNCTIONS VERSUS PATH FUNCTIONS
State Function
Path Function
State 2
U2
Total energy
ΔU = U2 – U1
–ΔU = U1 – U2
U1
State 1
Examples: d, P, V, T, U, H
Initial state
Ui
ΔU = heat
ΔU = heat + work
Uf
Final state
Examples: q, W

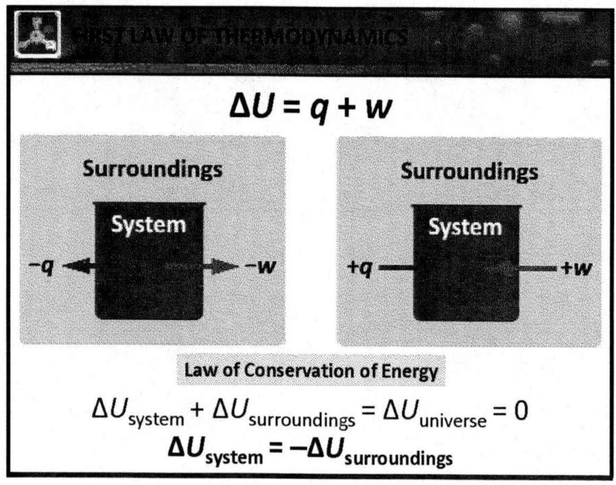
FIRST LAW OF THERMODYNAMICS
ΔU = q + w
Surroundings
System
−q
−w
Surroundings
System
+q
+w
Law of Conservation of Energy
ΔU_system + ΔU_surroundings = ΔU_universe = 0
ΔU_system = −ΔU_surroundings

CHECKPOINT

WORK VERSUS HEAT
COLD

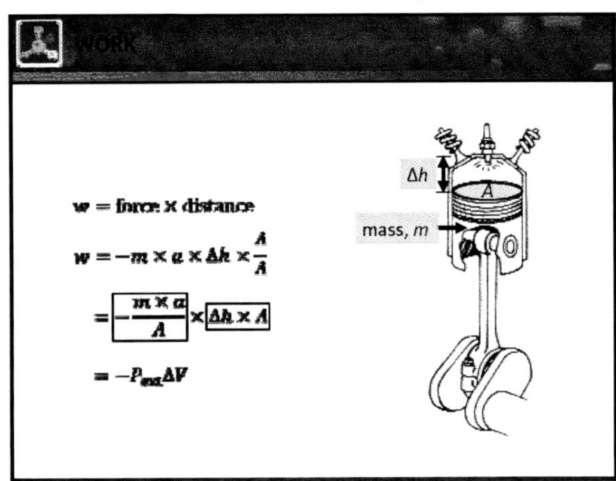
WORK
w = force × distance
w = −m × a × Δh × A/A
= −(m × a)/A × Δh × A
= −P_ext ΔV
Δh
A
mass, m

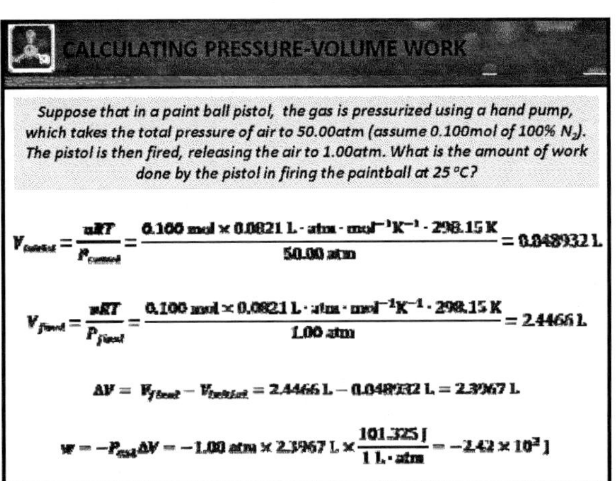
CALCULATING PRESSURE-VOLUME WORK
Suppose that in a paint ball pistol, the gas is pressurized using a hand pump, which takes the total pressure of air to 50.00atm (assume 0.100mol of 100% N₂). The pistol is then fired, releasing the air to 1.00atm. What is the amount of work done by the pistol in firing the paintball at 25 °C?
V_initial = nRT/P_current = (0.100 mol × 0.0821 L·atm·mol⁻¹K⁻¹·298.15 K)/(50.00 atm) = 0.048932 L
V_final = nRT/P_final = (0.100 mol × 0.0821 L·atm·mol⁻¹K⁻¹·298.15 K)/(1.00 atm) = 2.4466 L
ΔV = V_final − V_initial = 2.4466 L − 0.048932 L = 2.3967 L
w = −P_ext ΔV = −1.00 atm × 2.3967 L × 101.325 J/1 L·atm = −2.42 × 10² J

PRESSURE-VOLUME WORK FROM A CHEMICAL EQUATION

$$PV = nRT$$

$$w = -P_{ext}\Delta V$$

$$\Delta V = \Delta n\frac{RT}{P}$$

$$\therefore w = -P\Delta V = -\Delta n_{gases}RT$$

CHECKPOINT

MODULE 2

Thermochemistry II

HEAT CAPACITY

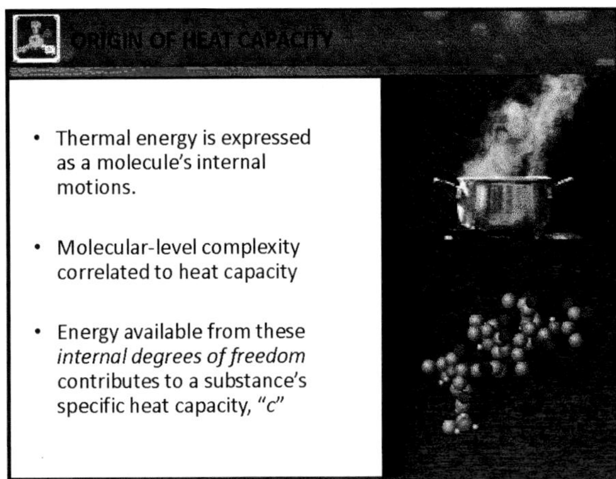
ORIGIN OF HEAT CAPACITY
Thermal energy is expressed as a molecule's internal motions.
Molecular-level complexity correlated to heat capacity
Energy available from these internal degrees of freedom contributes to a substance's specific heat capacity, "c"

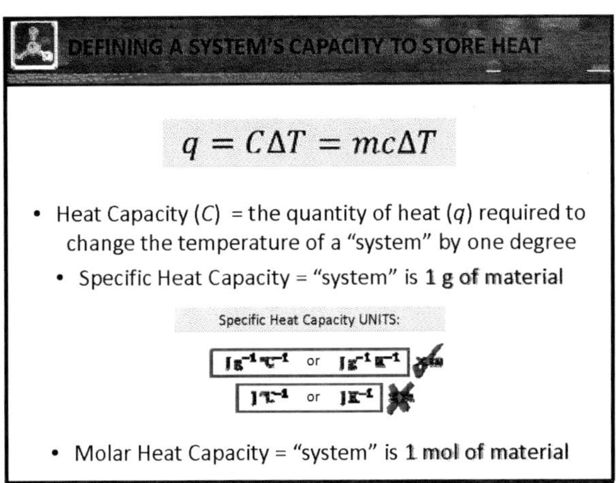
DEFINING A SYSTEM'S CAPACITY TO STORE HEAT
$q = C\Delta T = mc\Delta T$
Heat Capacity (C) = the quantity of heat (q) required to change the temperature of a "system" by one degree
Specific Heat Capacity = "system" is 1 g of material
Specific Heat Capacity UNITS:
$J\,g^{-1}\,°C^{-1}$ or $J\,g^{-1}\,K^{-1}$
$J\,°C^{-1}$ or $J\,K^{-1}$
Molar Heat Capacity = "system" is 1 mol of material

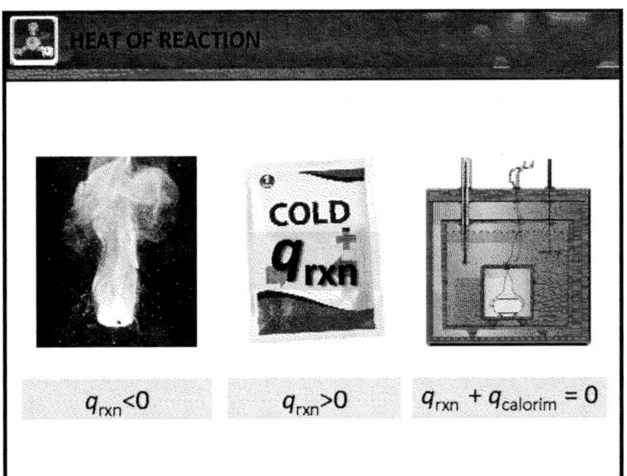
HEAT OF REACTION
COLD
q_{rxn}
$q_{rxn}<0$
$q_{rxn}>0$
$q_{rxn} + q_{calorim} = 0$

SAMPLE PROBLEM

A 100.0 g copper sample (specific heat = 0.385 J g^{-1} °C^{-1}) at 100.0 °C is added to 50.0 g water (specific heat = 4.184 J g^{-1} °C^{-1}), at 26.5 °C. What is the final temperature of the copper-water mixture?

Heat gained by water = Heat lost by copper

$$q_{(water)} = -q_{(copper)}$$

SOLUTION

$$m_{water} \times c_{water} \times (T_{final} - T_{initial(water)}) = -m_{copper} \times c_{copper} \times (T_{final} - T_{initial(copper)})$$

$$50.0\,g \times \frac{4.184\,J}{g\,°C} \times (T_f - 26.5\,°C) = -\left(100.0\,g \times \frac{0.385\,J}{g\,°C} \times (T_f - 100.0\,°C)\right)$$

$$209.2\frac{J}{°C}(T_f - 26.5\,°C) = -\left(38.5\frac{J}{°C} \times (T_f - 100.0\,°C)\right)$$

$$(209.2T_f - 5538.5\,°C) = -(38.5T_f - 3850\,°C)$$

$$5538.5\,°C + 3850\,°C = (209.2 + 38.5)T_f$$

$$T_f = \frac{9389\,°C}{247.7} = 37.9\,°C$$

CHECKPOINT

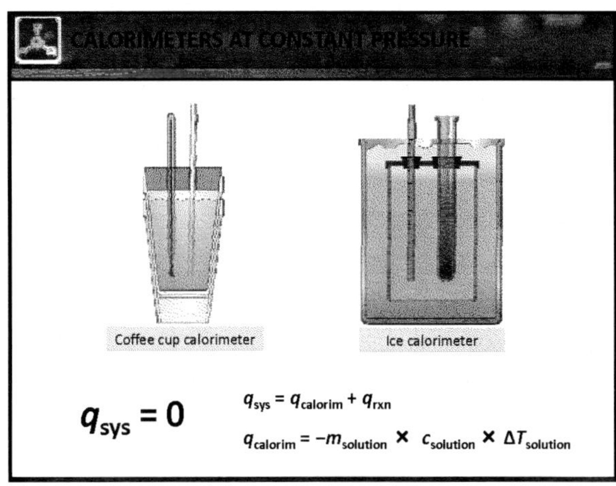

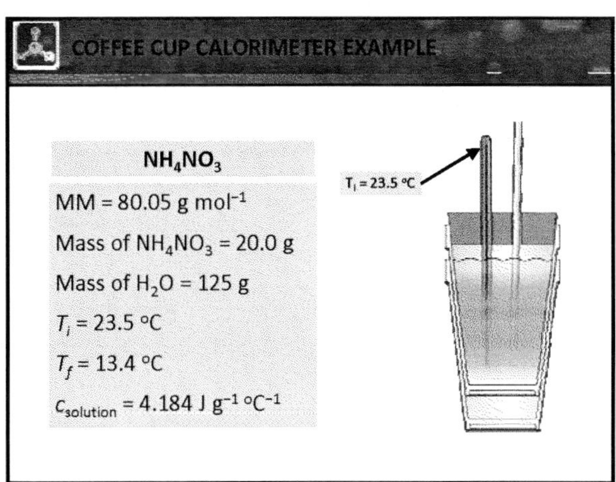

SOLUTION

$$q_{calorim} = m_{solution} \times c_{solution} \times \Delta T_{solution}$$

$$m_{solution} = m_{solvent} + m_{solute} = 125.0\,g + 20.0\,g$$

$$= 145.0\,g \times \frac{4.184\,J}{g\,°C} \times (13.4 - 23.5)\,°C$$

$$= -6.13\,kJ$$

$$q_{dissolution} = -q_{calorim}$$

$$\therefore q_{dissolution} = +6.13\,kJ$$

The <u>ions</u> gain energy, so the dissolution process is endothermic

TOTAL ENERGY, ΔU, AND ENTHALPY, ΔH

Total Energy & Enthalpy Closely Related

$$\Delta U = q + w = q_p - P\Delta V$$
$$q_p = \Delta U + P\Delta V$$

Definition of Enthalpy: $H = U + PV$

$$\Delta H = H_f - H_i = (U_f + P_f V_f) - (U_i + P_i V_i)$$
$$\Delta H = \Delta U + \Delta(PV)$$

If T & P are constant

$$\Delta H = \Delta U + P\Delta V$$
$$\boxed{\Delta H = q_p}$$

CHECKPOINT

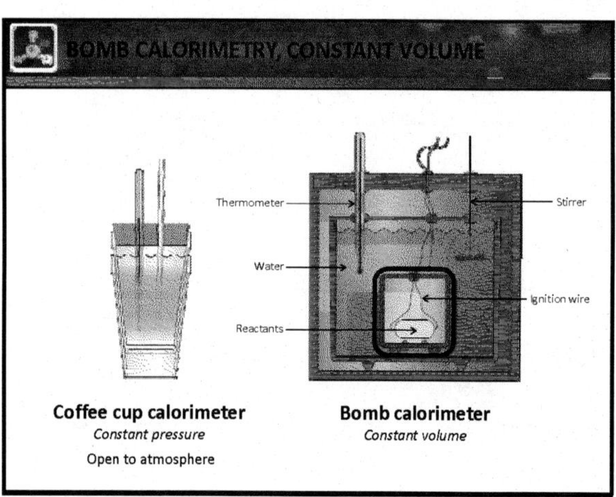

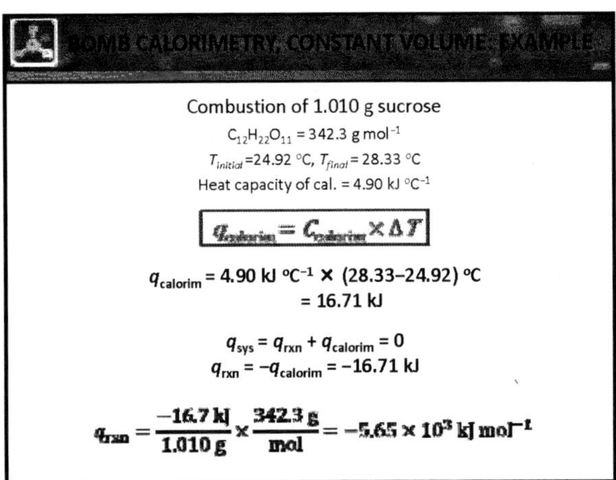
BOMB CALORIMETRY, CONSTANT VOLUME: EXAMPLE
Combustion of 1.010 g sucrose
$C_{12}H_{22}O_{11}$ = 342.3 g mol^{-1}
$T_{initial}$=24.92 °C, T_{final}= 28.33 °C
Heat capacity of cal. = 4.90 kJ °C^{-1}
$q_{calorim} = C_{calorim} \times \Delta T$
$q_{calorim}$ = 4.90 kJ °C^{-1} × (28.33–24.92) °C
= 16.71 kJ
$q_{sys} = q_{rxn} + q_{calorim} = 0$
$q_{rxn} = -q_{calorim} = -16.71$ kJ
$q_{rxn} = \frac{-16.7\text{ kJ}}{1.010\text{ g}} \times \frac{342.3\text{ g}}{\text{mol}} = -5.65 \times 10^3\text{ kJ mol}^{-1}$

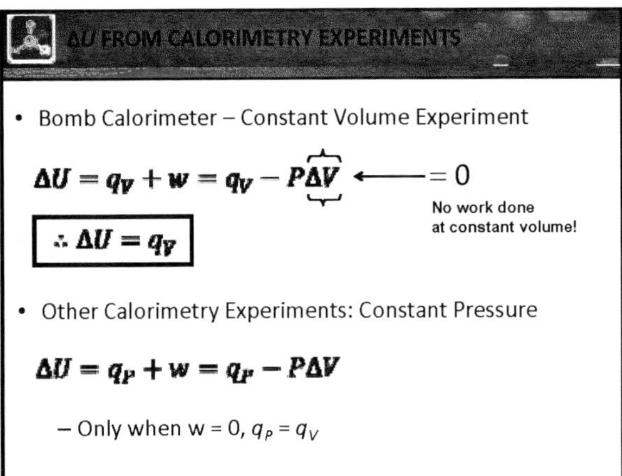
ΔU FROM CALORIMETRY EXPERIMENTS
• Bomb Calorimeter – Constant Volume Experiment
$\Delta U = q_V + w = q_V - P\Delta V$ ← = 0
No work done
at constant volume!
$\therefore \Delta U = q_V$
• Other Calorimetry Experiments: Constant Pressure
$\Delta U = q_P + w = q_P - P\Delta V$
– Only when w = 0, $q_P = q_V$

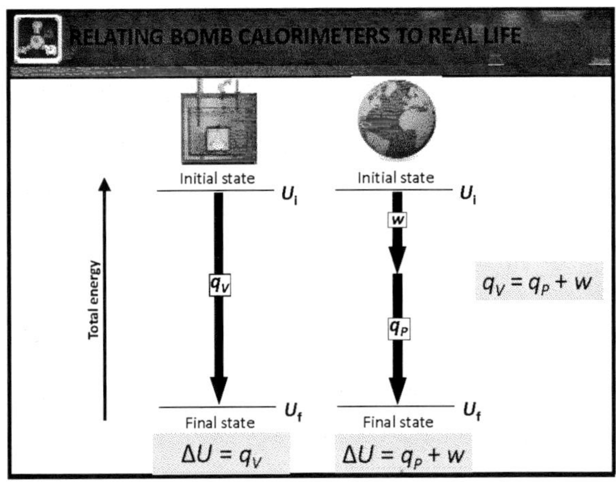
RELATING BOMB CALORIMETERS TO REAL LIFE
Initial state
U_i
Initial state
U_i
Total energy
q_V
w
q_P
$q_V = q_P + w$
Final state
U_f
Final state
U_f
$\Delta U = q_V$
$\Delta U = q_P + w$

ΔH FROM BOMB CALORIMETRY

$\therefore \Delta U = q_V$

If we know ΔU from a bomb calorimetry experiment, how can we find ΔH?

$\Delta U = q_V = q_P + w \quad \therefore w = -P\Delta V = -\Delta n_{gases}RT$

and $\Delta H = \Delta U + P\Delta V$

$= \Delta U + \Delta n_{gases}RT$

Thus, from the balanced chemical equation, we can find Δn, (change in # moles of gases) and solve for work, *w* at a given temperature. (see Tutorial)

RELATIONSHIPS BETWEEN ΔU, ΔH, q_P, q_V

$q_P = \Delta H = mc\Delta T = C\Delta T$

$w = -P\Delta V = -\Delta n_{gases}RT$

$\Delta U = q_P + w$

$\Delta U = q_V$

$\Delta H = \Delta U + \Delta n_{gases}RT$

CHECKPOINT

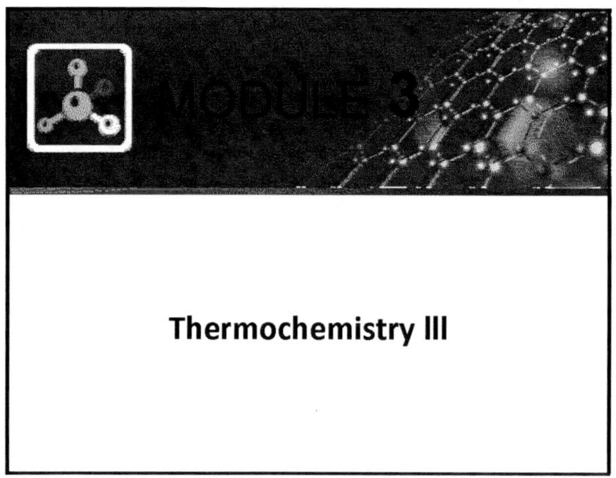
MODULE 3
Thermochemistry III

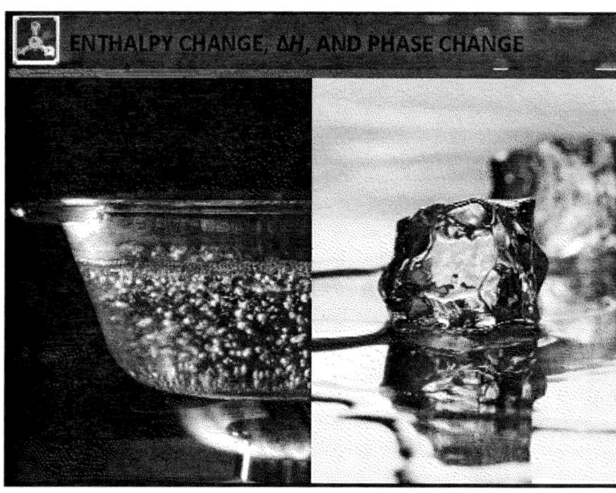
ENTHALPY CHANGE, ΔH, AND PHASE CHANGE

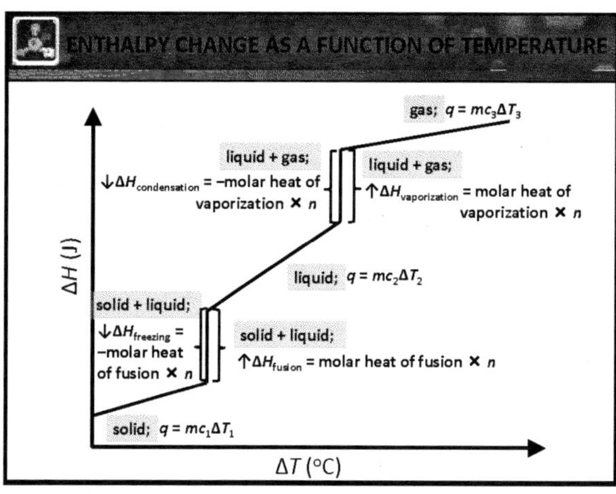
ENTHALPY CHANGE AS A FUNCTION OF TEMPERATURE
gas; $q = mc_3\Delta T_3$
liquid + gas;
$\downarrow \Delta H_{condensation}$ = −molar heat of vaporization × n
liquid + gas;
$\uparrow \Delta H_{vaporization}$ = molar heat of vaporization × n
liquid; $q = mc_2\Delta T_2$
solid + liquid;
$\downarrow \Delta H_{freezing}$ = −molar heat of fusion × n
solid + liquid;
$\uparrow \Delta H_{fusion}$ = molar heat of fusion × n
solid; $q = mc_1\Delta T_1$
ΔH (J)
ΔT (°C)

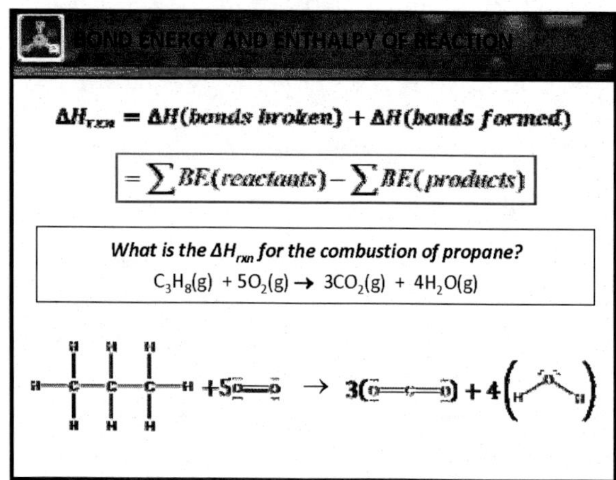
BOND ENERGY AND ENTHALPY OF REACTION
$\Delta H_{rxn} = \Delta H(bonds\ broken) + \Delta H(bonds\ formed)$
$= \sum BE(reactants) - \sum BE(products)$
What is the ΔH_{rxn} for the combustion of propane?
$C_3H_8(g) + 5O_2(g) \rightarrow 3CO_2(g) + 4H_2O(g)$

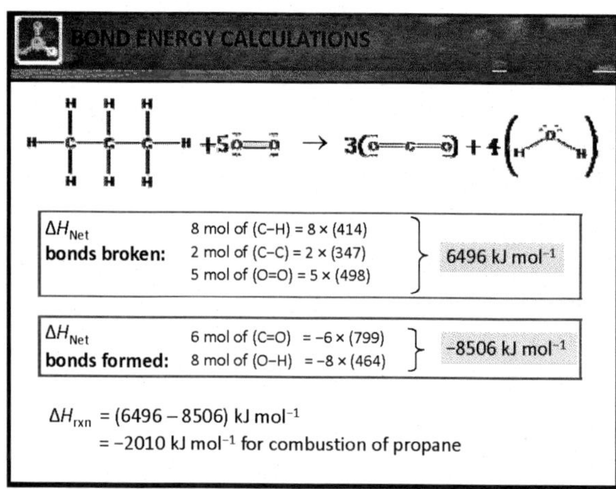
BOND ENERGY CALCULATIONS
ΔH_{Net} bonds broken:
8 mol of (C–H) = 8 × (414)
2 mol of (C–C) = 2 × (347)
5 mol of (O=O) = 5 × (498)
6496 kJ mol^{-1}
ΔH_{Net} bonds formed:
6 mol of (C=O) = −6 × (799)
8 mol of (O–H) = −8 × (464)
-8506 kJ mol^{-1}
ΔH_{rxn} = (6496 – 8506) kJ mol^{-1}
= −2010 kJ mol^{-1} for combustion of propane

CHECKPOINT

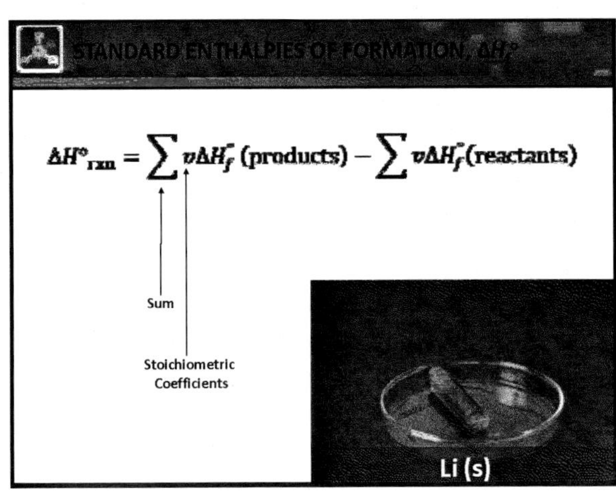
STANDARD ENTHALPIES OF FORMATION, ΔH°
$\Delta H^\circ_{rxn} = \sum v\Delta H_f^\circ (\text{products}) - \sum v\Delta H_f^\circ (\text{reactants})$
Sum
Stoichiometric Coefficients
Li (s)

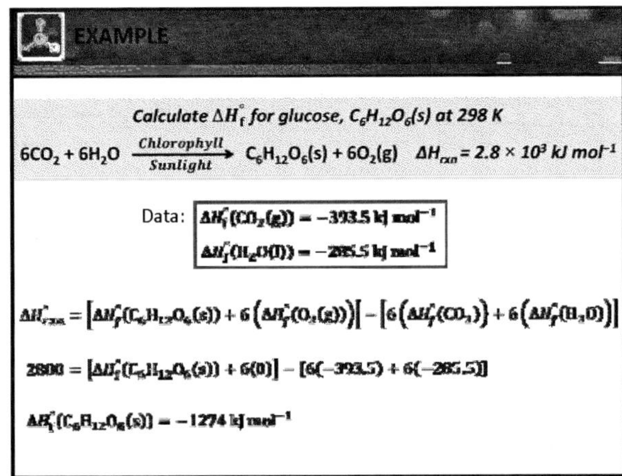
EXAMPLE
Calculate ΔH_f° for glucose, $C_6H_{12}O_6(s)$ at 298 K
$6CO_2 + 6H_2O \xrightarrow[Sunlight]{Chlorophyll} C_6H_{12}O_6(s) + 6O_2(g) \quad \Delta H_{rxn} = 2.8 \times 10^3$ kJ mol^{-1}
Data: $\Delta H_f^\circ(CO_2(g)) = -393.5$ kJ mol^{-1}
$\Delta H_f^\circ(H_2O(l)) = -285.5$ kJ mol^{-1}
$\Delta H_{rxn}^\circ = [\Delta H_f^\circ(C_6H_{12}O_6(s)) + 6(\Delta H_f^\circ(O_2(g)))] - [6(\Delta H_f^\circ(CO_2)) + 6(\Delta H_f^\circ(H_2O))]$
$2800 = [\Delta H_f^\circ(C_6H_{12}O_6(s)) + 6(0)] - [6(-393.5) + 6(-285.5)]$
$\Delta H_f^\circ(C_6H_{12}O_6(s)) = -1274$ kJ mol^{-1}

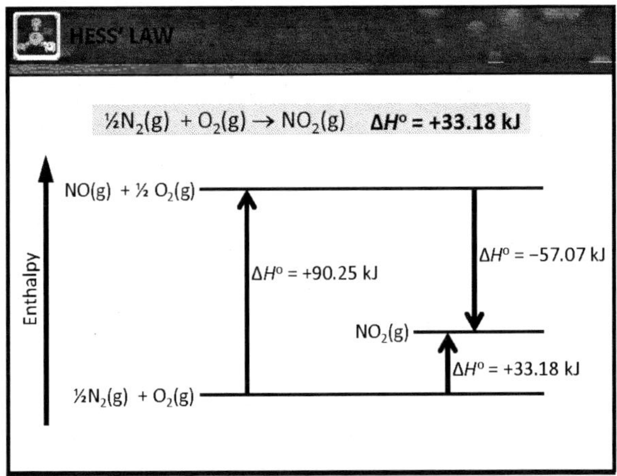
HESS' LAW
$\frac{1}{2}N_2(g) + O_2(g) \rightarrow NO_2(g) \quad \Delta H^\circ = +33.18$ kJ
Enthalpy
$NO(g) + \frac{1}{2} O_2(g)$
$\Delta H^\circ = +90.25$ kJ
$\Delta H^\circ = -57.07$ kJ
$NO_2(g)$
$\Delta H^\circ = +33.18$ kJ
$\frac{1}{2}N_2(g) + O_2(g)$

MANIPULATING THERMOCHEMISTRY EQUATIONS

$\frac{1}{2}N_2(g) + O_2(g) \rightarrow NO_2(g)$ $\Delta H^o = +33.18$ kJ

$\Delta H_f^o = 0$ kJ

$NO_2(g) \rightarrow \frac{1}{2}N_2(g) + O_2(g)$ $\Delta H^o = -33.18$ kJ

$\frac{1}{2}N_2(g) + \frac{1}{2}O_2(g) \rightarrow \cancel{NO(g)}$ $\Delta H^o = -90.25$ kJ

$\cancel{NO(g)} + \frac{1}{2}O_2(g) \rightarrow NO_2(g)$ $\Delta H^o = -57.07$ kJ

$\frac{1}{2}N_2(g) + O_2(g) \rightarrow NO_2(g)$ $\Delta H^o = +33.18$ kJ

2 × $[\frac{1}{2}N_2(g) + O_2(g) \rightarrow NO_2(g)]$ ($\Delta H^o = +33.18$ kJ) **× 2**

$N_2(g) + \mathbf{2}O_2(g) \rightarrow \mathbf{2}NO_2(g)$ $\Delta H^o = +\mathbf{66.36}$ kJ

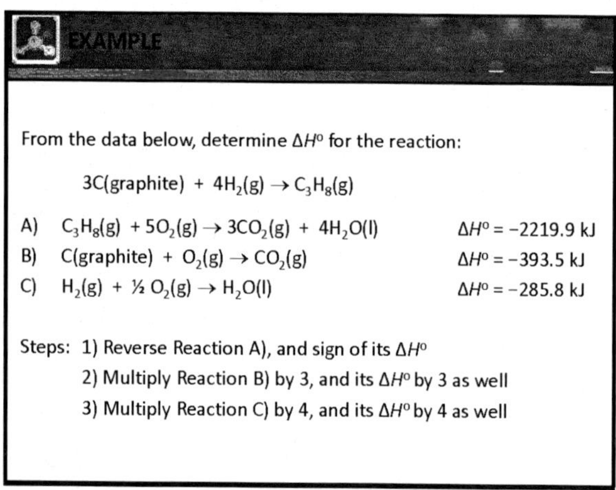

EXAMPLE
From the data below, determine ΔH° for the reaction:
3C(graphite) + 4H2(g) → C3H8(g)
A) C3H8(g) + 5O2(g) → 3CO2(g) + 4H2O(l) ΔH° = −2219.9 kJ
B) C(graphite) + O2(g) → CO2(g) ΔH° = −393.5 kJ
C) H2(g) + ½ O2(g) → H2O(l) ΔH° = −285.8 kJ
Steps: 1) Reverse Reaction A), and sign of its ΔH°
2) Multiply Reaction B) by 3, and its ΔH° by 3 as well
3) Multiply Reaction C) by 4, and its ΔH° by 4 as well

SOLUTION

Reverse A)

$3\cancel{CO_2(g)} + 4\cancel{H_2O(l)} \rightarrow C_3H_8(g) + \cancel{5O_2(g)}$ $\Delta H^o = +2219.9$ kJ

3 × B)

$3C(graphite) + \cancel{3O_2(g)} \rightarrow \cancel{3CO_2(g)}$ $\Delta H^o = 3 \times (-393.5$ kJ$)$

4 × C)

$4H_2(g) + \cancel{4(\frac{1}{2})O_2(g)} \rightarrow \cancel{4H_2O(l)}$ $\Delta H^o = 4 \times (-285.8$ kJ$)$

$3C(graphite) + 4H_2(g) \rightarrow C_3H_8(g)$

$\Delta H^o = [2219.9 + 3(-393.5) + 4(-285.8)]$ kJ
$= -103.8$ kJ

CHECKPOINT

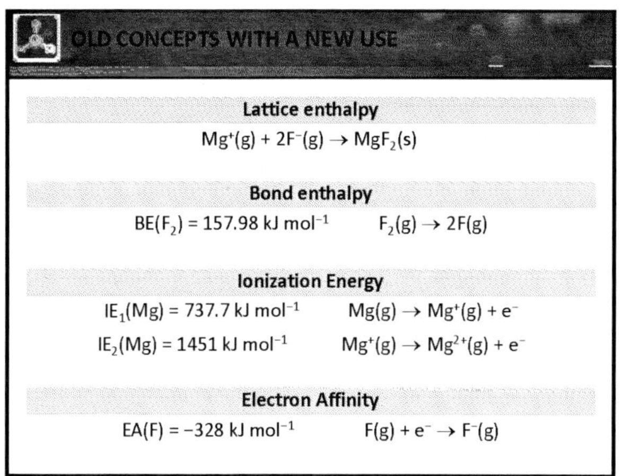
OLD CONCEPTS WITH A NEW USE
Lattice enthalpy
$Mg^{+}(g) + 2F^{-}(g) \rightarrow MgF_2(s)$
Bond enthalpy
$BE(F_2) = 157.98$ kJ mol^{-1}
$F_2(g) \rightarrow 2F(g)$
Ionization Energy
$IE_1(Mg) = 737.7$ kJ mol^{-1}
$Mg(g) \rightarrow Mg^{+}(g) + e^{-}$
$IE_2(Mg) = 1451$ kJ mol^{-1}
$Mg^{+}(g) \rightarrow Mg^{2+}(g) + e^{-}$
Electron Affinity
$EA(F) = -328$ kJ mol^{-1}
$F(g) + e^{-} \rightarrow F^{-}(g)$

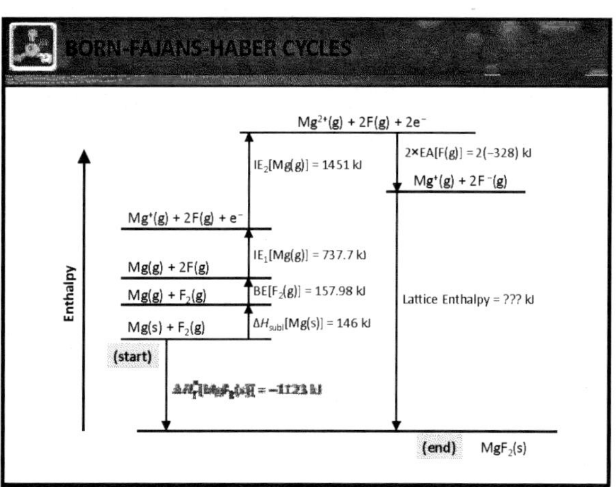
BORN-FAJANS-HABER CYCLES
$Mg^{2+}(g) + 2F(g) + 2e^{-}$
$IE_2[Mg(g)] = 1451$ kJ
$2\times EA[F(g)] = 2(-328)$ kJ
$Mg^{+}(g) + 2F^{-}(g)$
$Mg^{+}(g) + 2F(g) + e^{-}$
$IE_1[Mg(g)] = 737.7$ kJ
$Mg(g) + 2F(g)$
$BE[F_2(g)] = 157.98$ kJ
$Mg(g) + F_2(g)$
$\Delta H_{subl}[Mg(s)] = 146$ kJ
$Mg(s) + F_2(g)$
Enthalpy
Lattice Enthalpy = ??? kJ
(start)
= −1123 kJ
(end)
$MgF_2(s)$

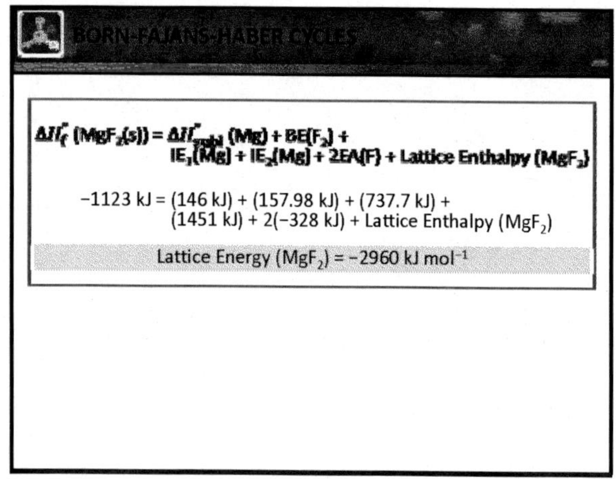
BORN-FAJANS-HABER CYCLES
$\Delta H_f^\circ (MgF_2(s)) = \Delta H_{sub}^\circ (Mg) + BE(F_2) + IE_1(Mg) + IE_2(Mg) + 2EA(F) + \text{Lattice Enthalpy} (MgF_2)$
$-1123\ kJ = (146\ kJ) + (157.98\ kJ) + (737.7\ kJ) + (1451\ kJ) + 2(-328\ kJ) + \text{Lattice Enthalpy} (MgF_2)$
Lattice Energy (MgF_2) = $-2960\ kJ\ mol^{-1}$

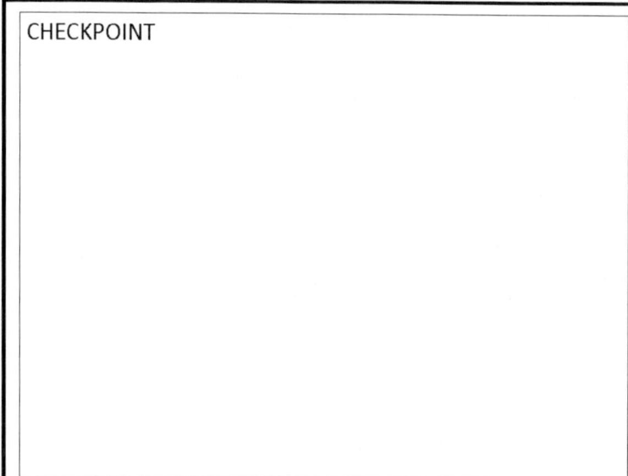
CHECKPOINT

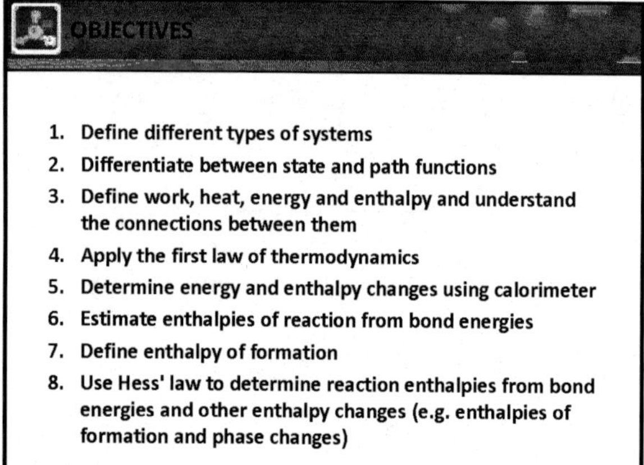
OBJECTIVES
1. Define different types of systems
2. Differentiate between state and path functions
3. Define work, heat, energy and enthalpy and understand the connections between them
4. Apply the first law of thermodynamics
5. Determine energy and enthalpy changes using calorimeter
6. Estimate enthalpies of reaction from bond energies
7. Define enthalpy of formation
8. Use Hess' law to determine reaction enthalpies from bond energies and other enthalpy changes (e.g. enthalpies of formation and phase changes)

Unit 8

Most important concepts:

-
-
-
-
-
-
-
-
-
-
-
-

Unit 8

Questions I have:

-
-
-
-
-
-
-
-
-
-
-
-

UNIT 9 – Entropy and Free Energy

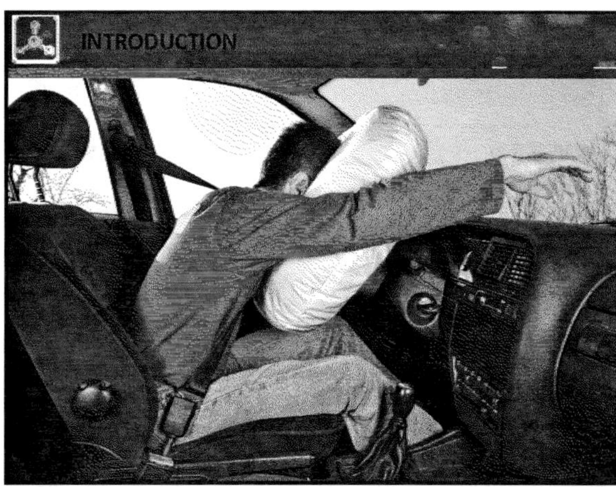

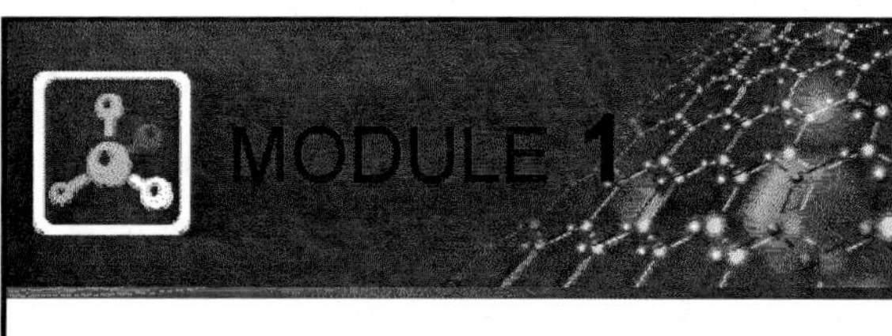

Entropy and Free Energy I

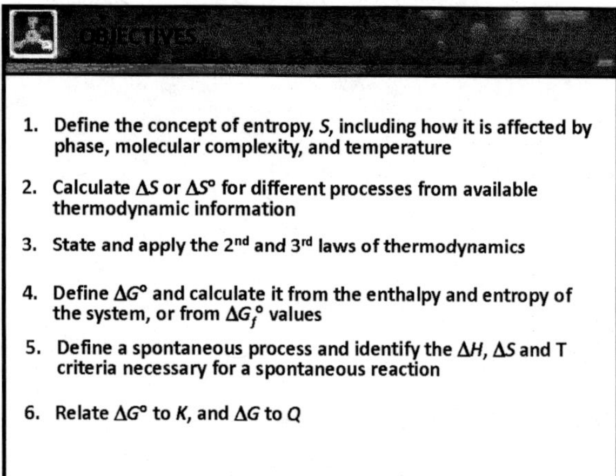
OBJECTIVES
1. Define the concept of entropy, S, including how it is affected by phase, molecular complexity, and temperature
2. Calculate ΔS or ΔS° for different processes from available thermodynamic information
3. State and apply the 2nd and 3rd laws of thermodynamics
4. Define ΔG° and calculate it from the enthalpy and entropy of the system, or from ΔGf° values
5. Define a spontaneous process and identify the ΔH, ΔS and T criteria necessary for a spontaneous reaction
6. Relate ΔG° to K, and ΔG to Q

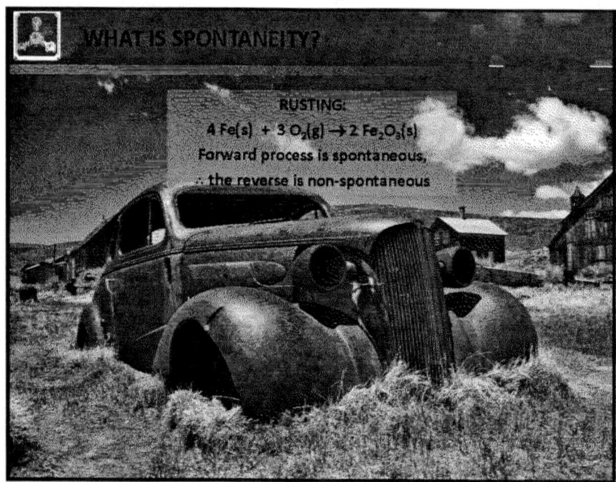
WHAT IS SPONTANEITY?
RUSTING:
4 Fe(s) + 3 O2(g) → 2 Fe2O3(s)
Forward process is spontaneous,
∴ the reverse is non-spontaneous

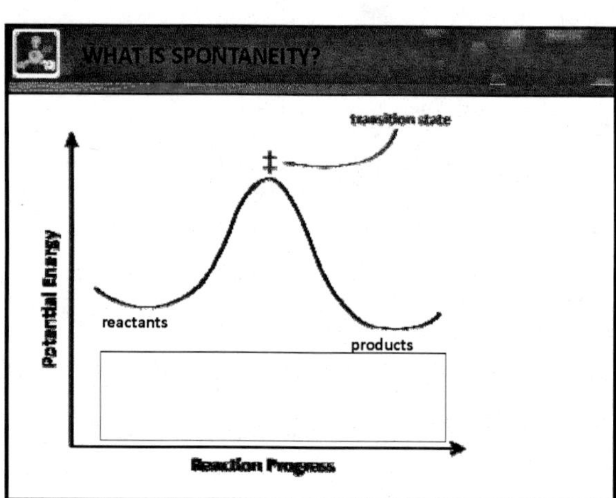
WHAT IS SPONTANEITY?
transition state
‡
Potential Energy
reactants
products
Reaction Progress

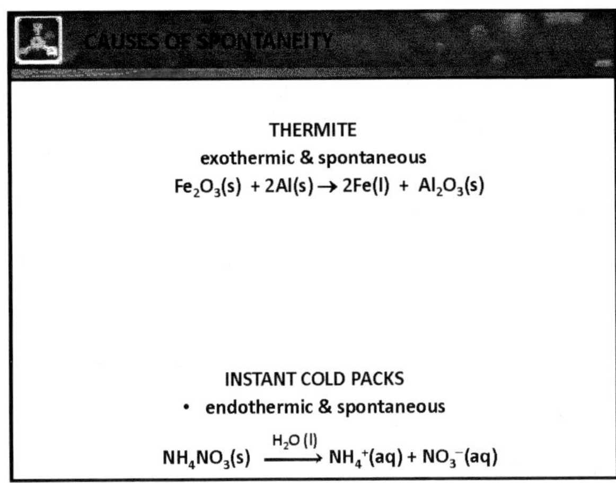
CAUSES OF SPONTANEITY
THERMITE
exothermic & spontaneous
$Fe_2O_3(s) + 2Al(s) \rightarrow 2Fe(l) + Al_2O_3(s)$
INSTANT COLD PACKS
• endothermic & spontaneous
$NH_4NO_3(s) \xrightarrow{H_2O(l)} NH_4^+(aq) + NO_3^-(aq)$

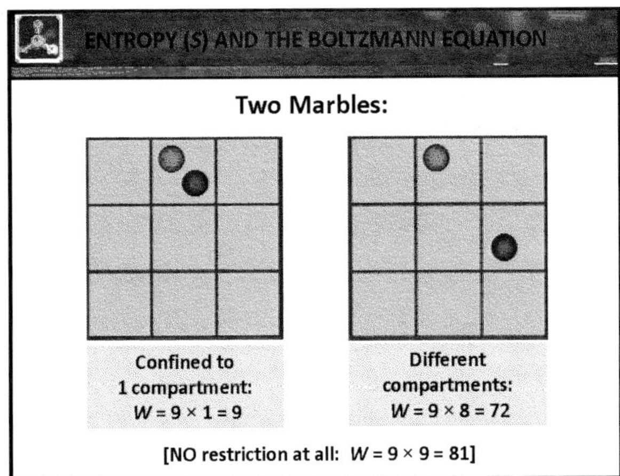
ENTROPY (S) AND THE BOLTZMANN EQUATION
Two Marbles:
Confined to 1 compartment: $W = 9 \times 1 = 9$
Different compartments: $W = 9 \times 8 = 72$
[NO restriction at all: $W = 9 \times 9 = 81$]

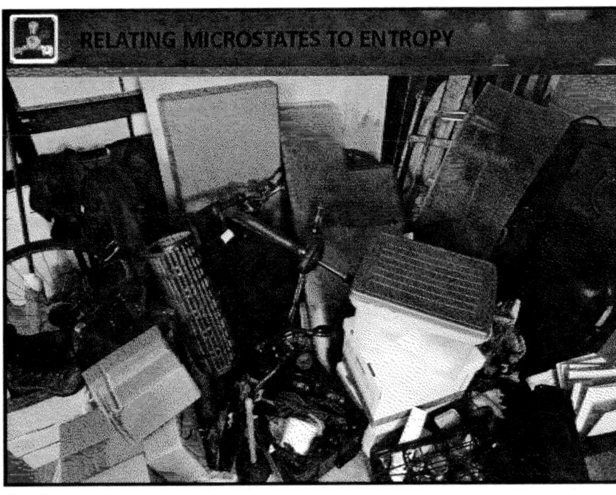
RELATING MICROSTATES TO ENTROPY

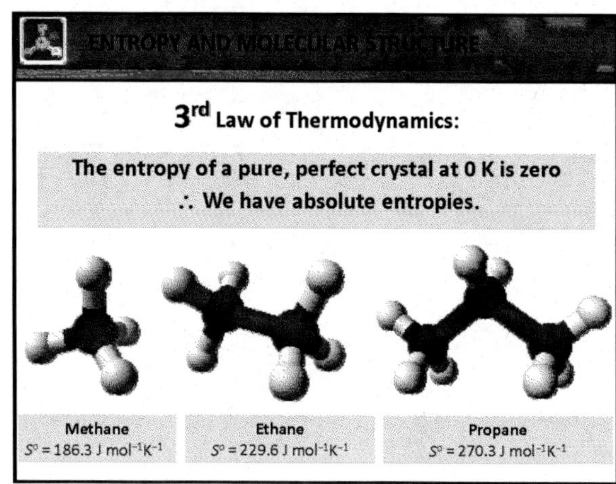
ENTROPY AND MOLECULAR STRUCTURE
3rd Law of Thermodynamics:
The entropy of a pure, perfect crystal at 0 K is zero
∴ We have absolute entropies.
Methane
$S° = 186.3$ J mol^{-1}K^{-1}
Ethane
$S° = 229.6$ J mol^{-1}K^{-1}
Propane
$S° = 270.3$ J mol^{-1}K^{-1}

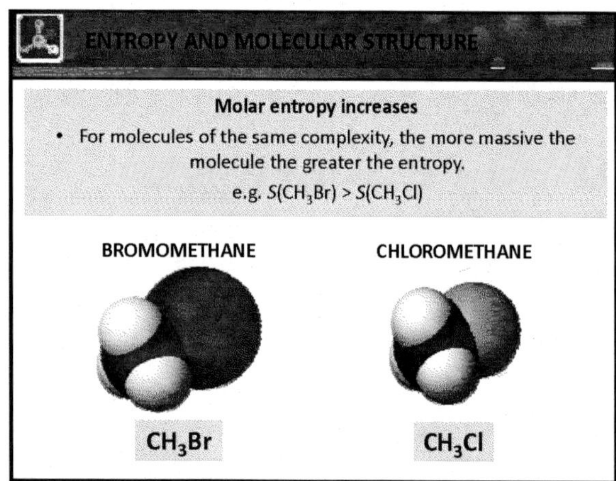
ENTROPY AND MOLECULAR STRUCTURE
Molar entropy increases
• For molecules of the same complexity, the more massive the molecule the greater the entropy.
e.g. $S(CH_3Br) > S(CH_3Cl)$
BROMOMETHANE
CHLOROMETHANE
CH_3Br
CH_3Cl

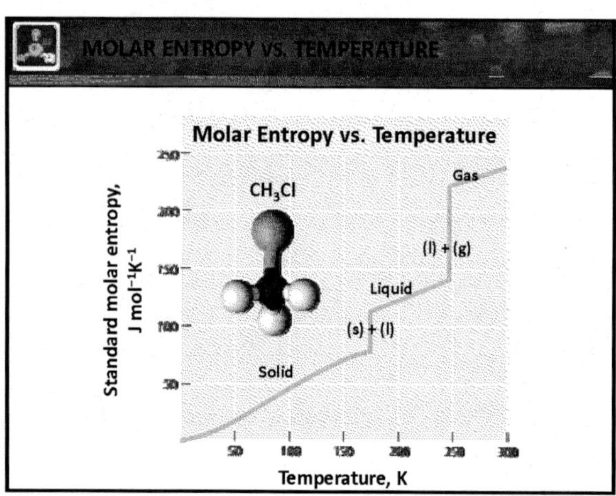
MOLAR ENTROPY VS. TEMPERATURE
Molar Entropy vs. Temperature
CH_3Cl
Gas
(l) + (g)
Liquid
(s) + (l)
Solid
Standard molar entropy, J mol^{-1}K^{-1}
Temperature, K

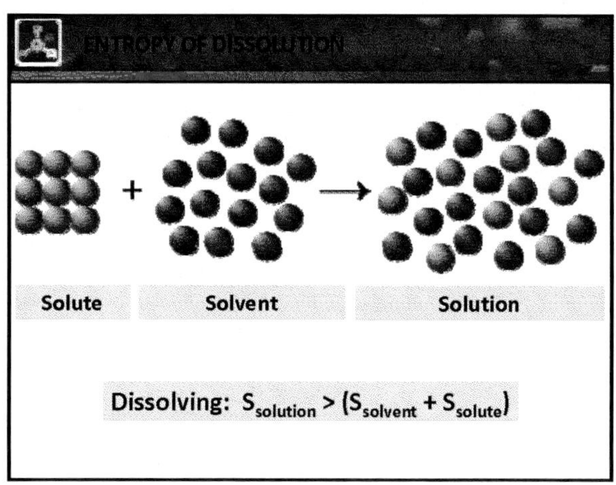
ENTROPY OF DISSOLUTION
Solute
Solvent
Solution
Dissolving: S_solution > (S_solvent + S_solute)

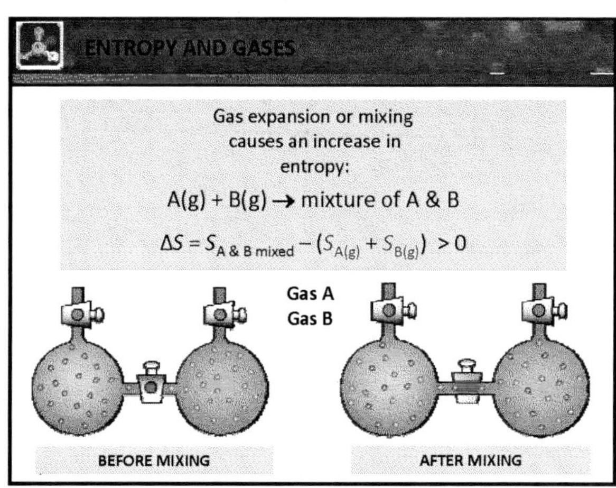
ENTROPY AND GASES
Gas expansion or mixing causes an increase in entropy:
A(g) + B(g) → mixture of A & B
ΔS = S_A & B mixed − (S_A(g) + S_B(g)) > 0
Gas A
Gas B
BEFORE MIXING
AFTER MIXING

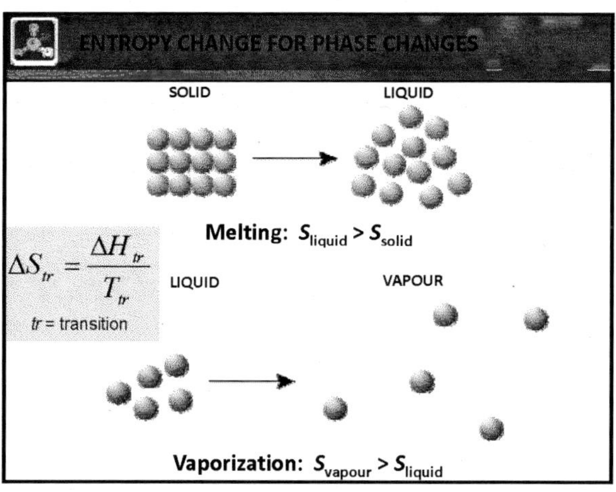
ENTROPY CHANGE FOR PHASE CHANGES
SOLID
LIQUID
Melting: S_liquid > S_solid
ΔS_tr = ΔH_tr / T_tr
tr = transition
LIQUID
VAPOUR
Vaporization: S_vapour > S_liquid

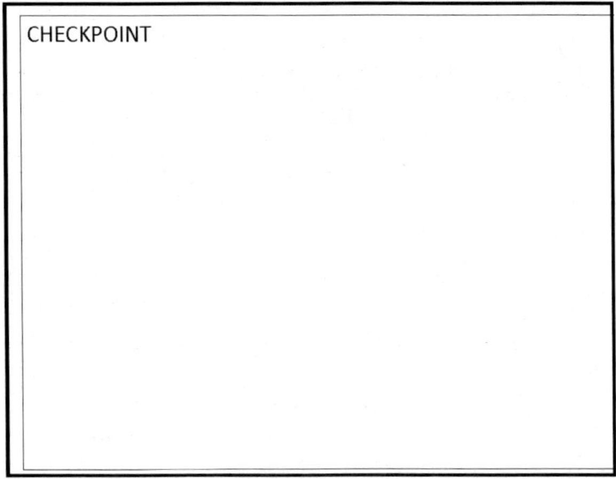
CHECKPOINT

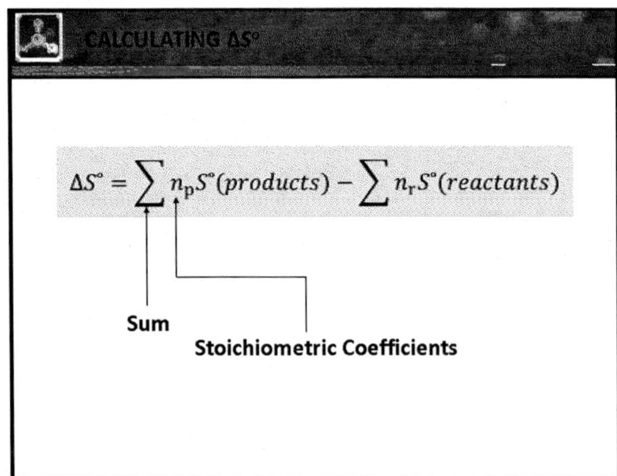
CALCULATING ΔS°
$\Delta S^\circ = \sum n_p S^\circ(products) - \sum n_r S^\circ(reactants)$
Sum
Stoichiometric Coefficients

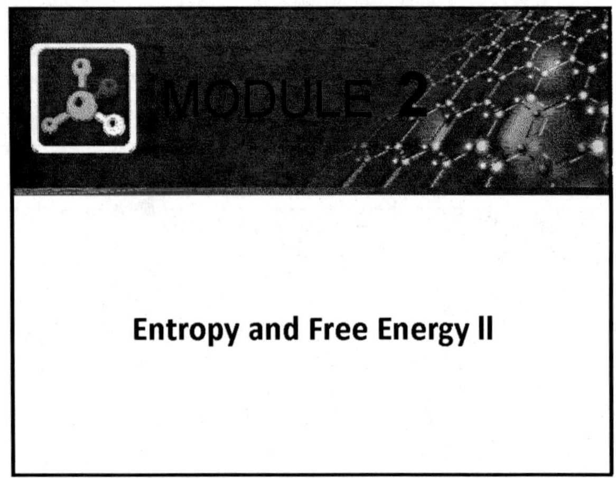
MODULE 2
Entropy and Free Energy II

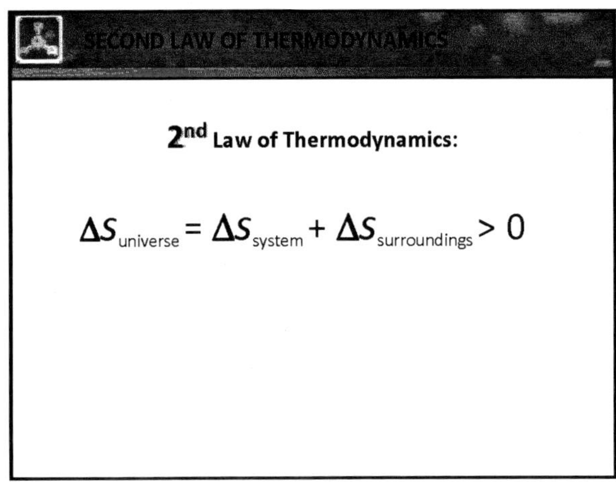

SECOND LAW OF THERMODYNAMICS
2nd Law of Thermodynamics:
ΔS universe = ΔS system + ΔS surroundings > 0

SECOND LAW OF THERMODYNAMICS IN PRACTICE

$\Delta S_{universe}$ & an $H_2 + O_2$ Balloon

$H_2(g) + \frac{1}{2} O_2(g) \rightarrow H_2O(l)$

- Reaction will be exothermic and ΔS_{sys} will be negative

$$\Delta S^\circ_{rxn} = \sum n_p S^\circ(\text{products}) - \sum n_r S^\circ(\text{reactants})$$

$$\Delta S^\circ_{rxn} = 1\text{ mol} \times 69.91\text{ J mol}^{-1}\text{ K}^{-1} - (1\text{ mol} \times 130.7\text{ J mol}^{-1}\text{ K}^{-1} + \tfrac{1}{2}\text{ mol} \times 205.1\text{ J mol}^{-1}\text{ K}^{-1})$$

$$\Delta S^\circ_{rxn} = -163.3\text{ J mol}^{-1}\text{ K}^{-1}$$

$$\Delta S^\circ_{rxn} = \Delta S^\circ_{sys}\ (\text{entropy decreases})$$

CALCULATING $\Delta S_{surroundings}$

What about $\Delta S_{surroundings}$?

$$q_{surr} = -q_{sys} = -\Delta H_{sys}$$

$$\boxed{\Delta S_{surr}} = \frac{-q_{surroundings}}{T} = \frac{-\Delta H_{sys}}{T}$$

← Substituting this into the 2nd Law, $\Delta S_{univ} = \Delta S_{sys} + \boxed{\Delta S_{surr}}$

$$\Delta S_{universe} = \Delta S_{system} - \boxed{\frac{\Delta H_{system}}{T}}$$

Now back to the H_2/O_2 Balloon...

Note: spontaneity is predicted based on properties of the SYSTEM only.

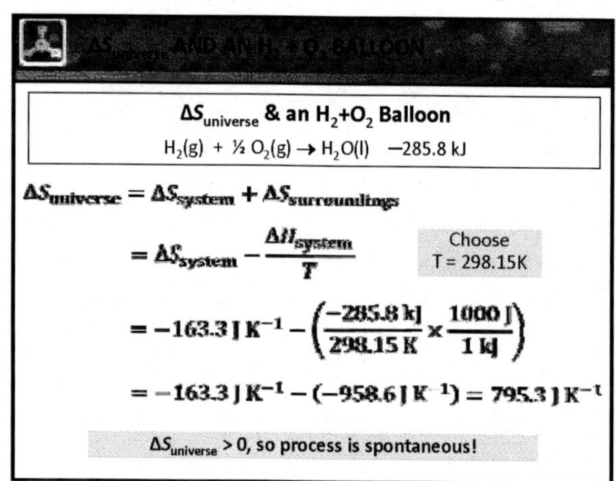

$\Delta S_{universe}$ AND AN $H_2 + O_2$ BALLOON
$\Delta S_{universe}$ & an H_2+O_2 Balloon
$H_2(g) + \frac{1}{2} O_2(g) \rightarrow H_2O(l)$ −285.8 kJ
$\Delta S_{universe} = \Delta S_{system} + \Delta S_{surroundings}$
$= \Delta S_{system} - \frac{\Delta H_{system}}{T}$
Choose T = 298.15K
$= -163.3\ \mathrm{J\,K^{-1}} - \left(\frac{-285.8\ \mathrm{kJ}}{298.15\ \mathrm{K}} \times \frac{1000\ \mathrm{J}}{1\ \mathrm{kJ}}\right)$
$= -163.3\ \mathrm{J\,K^{-1}} - (-958.6\ \mathrm{J\,K^{-1}}) = 795.3\ \mathrm{J\,K^{-1}}$
$\Delta S_{universe} > 0$, so process is spontaneous!

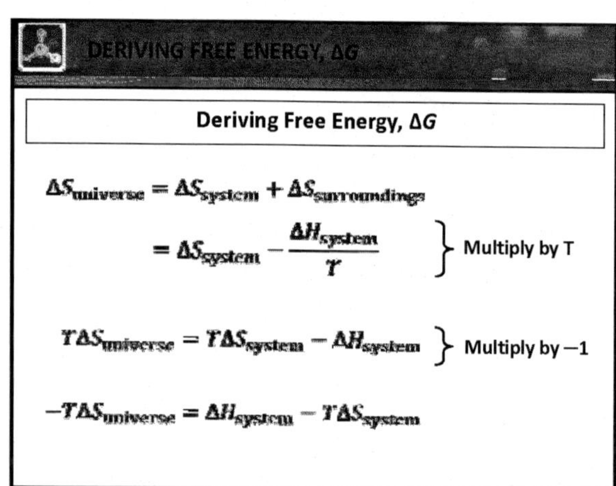

DERIVING FREE ENERGY, ΔG
Deriving Free Energy, ΔG
$\Delta S_{universe} = \Delta S_{system} + \Delta S_{surroundings}$
$= \Delta S_{system} - \frac{\Delta H_{system}}{T}$
Multiply by T
$T\Delta S_{universe} = T\Delta S_{system} - \Delta H_{system}$
Multiply by −1
$-T\Delta S_{universe} = \Delta H_{system} - T\Delta S_{system}$

FREE ENERGY, ΔG

Free Energy, ΔG

$$-T\Delta S_{universe} = \Delta H_{system} - T\Delta S_{system}$$

$\Delta S_{univ} > 0$ For Spontaneous Processes

All terms for System Only

$$\Delta G = -T\Delta S_{universe}$$

Criterion for Spontaneous Change: Negative Change in Free Energy, ΔG

$$\Delta G = \Delta H - T\Delta S$$

Free Energy, G
A State Function of the System

SUMMARY OF CRITERIA FOR SPONTANEOUS CHANGE

$$\Delta G = \Delta H - T\Delta S$$

	ΔH	ΔS	ΔG	Result	Example
1.	-	+	-	Spontaneous All Temp	$2NI_3(s) \rightarrow N_2(g) + 3I_2(s)$ (feather-induced explosion!)
2.	-	-	- +	Spon. Low T Non-Spon. High T	$H_2O(l) \rightarrow H_2O(s)$
3.	+	+	+ -	Non-Spon. Low T Spon. High T	$NH_4NO_3(s) \rightarrow NH_4NO_3(aq)$
4.	+	-	+	Non-Spontaneous All Temp	$3O_2(g) \rightarrow 2O_3(g)$

CHECKPOINT

FREE ENERGY AND PHASE TRANSITIONS

Transition Temperature, and ΔG

Recall: $\Delta S_{tr} = \dfrac{\Delta H_{tr}}{T_{tr}}$

For a phase transition, $\Delta G = 0$
i.e. $\Delta G_{tr} = \Delta H_{tr} - T\Delta S_{tr} = 0$ if $T = T_{tr}$

Example:

Consider melting (**fusion**) for which $\Delta H > 0$ and $\Delta S > 0$.

$\Delta G_{fus} = \Delta H_{fus} - T\Delta S_{fus} < 0$ if $T > T_m$

i.e. melting is **spontaneous above** the melting point

$\Delta G_{fus} = \Delta H_{fus} - T\Delta S_{fus} > 0$ if $T < T_m$

i.e. melting is **nonspontaneous below** the melting point

STANDARD FREE ENERGY CHANGE, ΔG°

Standard Free Energy Change, $\Delta G°$

$$\Delta G° = \Delta H° - T\Delta S°$$

Calculations follow strategies used for $\Delta H°$ and $\Delta S°$

$$\Delta G^{\circ}_{rxn} = \sum n_p \Delta G^{\circ}_f(products) - \sum n_r \Delta G^{\circ}_f(reactants)$$

ΔG UNDER NON-STANDARD CONDITIONS

$$\text{Reactants} \overset{K}{\rightleftharpoons} \text{Products}$$

$$\boxed{\Delta G^{\circ} = -RT\ln K}$$

$$\Delta G = \Delta G^{\circ} + RT\ln Q$$

$$E_{cell} = E^{\circ}_{cell} - \frac{RT}{zF}\ln Q$$

OBJECTIVES

1. Define the concept of entropy, S, including how it is affected by phase, molecular complexity, and temperature
2. Calculate ΔS or $\Delta S°$ for different processes from available thermodynamic information
3. State and apply the 2nd and 3rd laws of thermodynamics
4. Define $\Delta G°$ and calculate it from the enthalpy and entropy of the system, or from $\Delta G_f°$ values
5. Define a spontaneous process and identify the ΔH, ΔS and T criteria necessary for a spontaneous reaction
6. Relate $\Delta G°$ to K, and ΔG to Q

Unit 9

Most important concepts:

-
-
-
-
-
-
-
-
-
-
-
-

Unit 9

Questions I have:

-
-
-
-
-
-
-
-
-
-
-
-

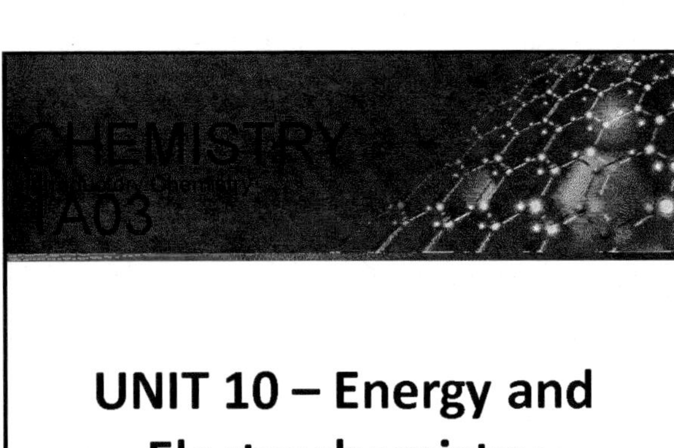

UNIT 10 – Energy and Electrochemistry

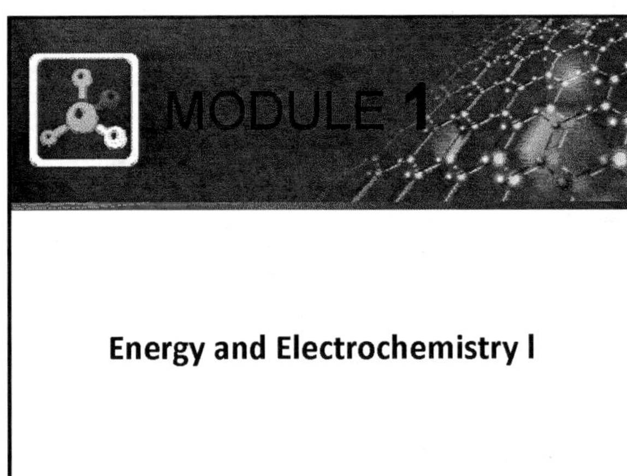

Energy and Electrochemistry I

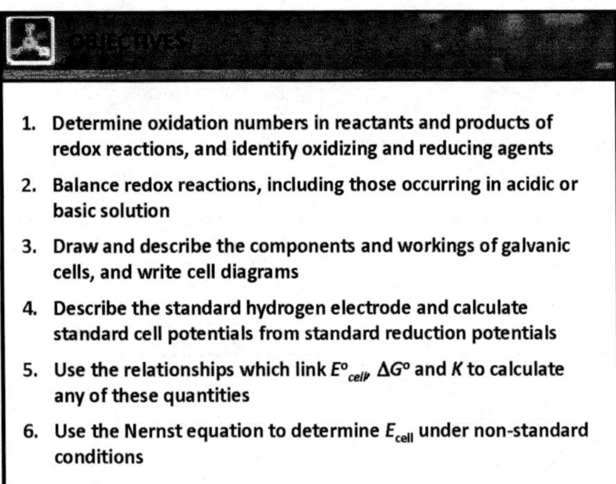
OBJECTIVES
1. Determine oxidation numbers in reactants and products of redox reactions, and identify oxidizing and reducing agents
2. Balance redox reactions, including those occurring in acidic or basic solution
3. Draw and describe the components and workings of galvanic cells, and write cell diagrams
4. Describe the standard hydrogen electrode and calculate standard cell potentials from standard reduction potentials
5. Use the relationships which link E°_{cell}, ΔG° and K to calculate any of these quantities
6. Use the Nernst equation to determine E_{cell} under non-standard conditions

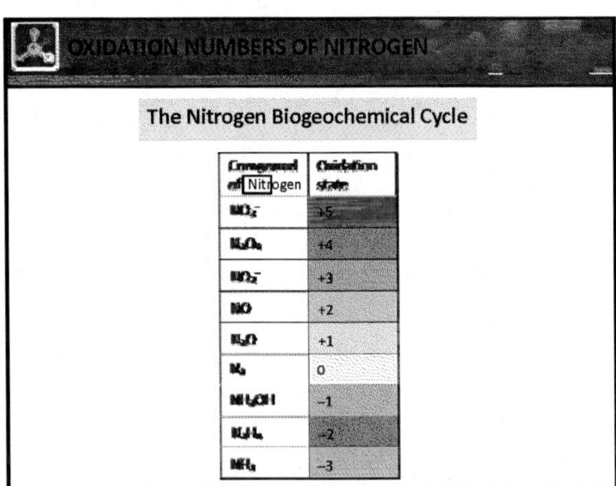
OXIDATION NUMBERS OF NITROGEN
The Nitrogen Biogeochemical Cycle
Nitrogen
+5
+4
+3
+2
+1
0
−1
−2
−3

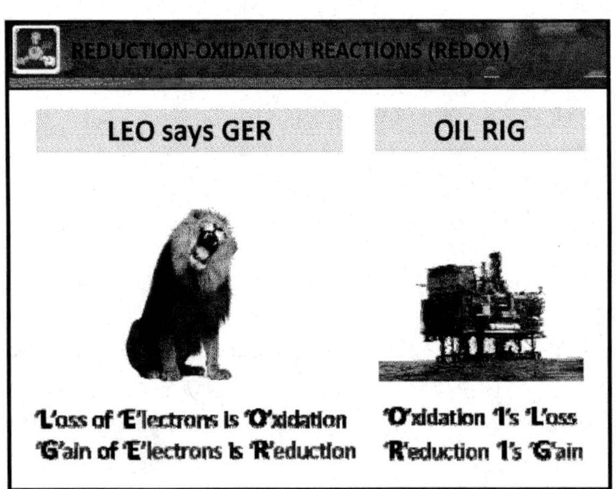
REDUCTION-OXIDATION REACTIONS (REDOX)
LEO says GER
OIL RIG
'L'oss of 'E'lectrons is 'O'xidation
'G'ain of 'E'lectrons is 'R'eduction
'O'xidation 'I's 'L'oss
'R'eduction 'I's 'G'ain

REDOX REACTIONS AND TERMINOLOGY

Thermite Reaction Equation:

Oxidizing agent **Reducing agent**

$Fe_2O_3(s) + 2Al(s) \rightarrow 2Fe(l) + Al_2O_3(s)$

+3 0 0 +3

Half Reactions:

$Fe^{3+}(s) + 3e^- \rightarrow Fe(l)$ **Reduction (Gains e^-)**

$Al(s) \rightarrow Al^{3+}(s) + 3e^-$ **Oxidation (Loses e^-)**

T > 2,000 K Highly Exothermic!

CHECKPOINT

BALANCING REDOX REACTIONS

1. Deduce the **oxidation numbers** for all species → This will identify the oxidizing and reducing agents
2. Write reduction and oxidation skeleton **half-reactions**
3. **Balance** the redox atoms (usually not O, H unless they are participating in the redox chemistry)
4. Add the correct number of **electrons** to each half-reaction

5a. If **acidic conditions:** Balance O by adding H_2O then H by H^+

5b. If **basic conditions:** Balance as if in acidic conditions, then add OH^- to balance the H^+ (making water), then cancel the H_2O (or balance the negative charges by adding OH^-, then balance O & H by adding H_2O)

6. **Check atoms and charges**. Multiply half-reactions by a factor, if needed, to make the number of electrons transferred match.
7. **Write the net redox reaction!**

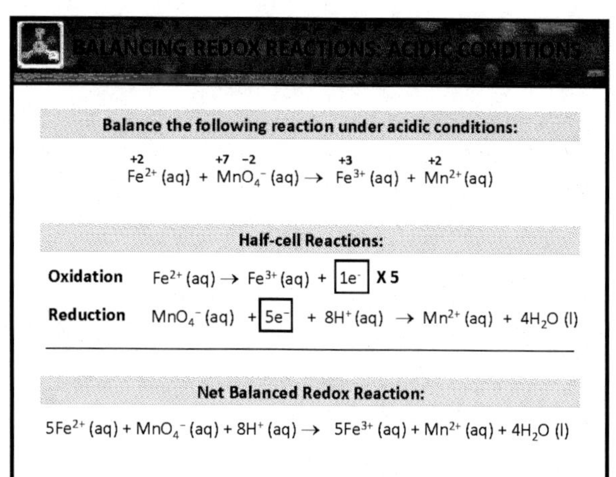

BALANCING REDOX REACTIONS: ACIDIC CONDITIONS
Balance the following reaction under acidic conditions:
$\overset{+2}{Fe}{}^{2+}(aq) + \overset{+7}{Mn}\overset{-2}{O}{}_4^-(aq) \rightarrow \overset{+3}{Fe}{}^{3+}(aq) + \overset{+2}{Mn}{}^{2+}(aq)$
Half-cell Reactions:
Oxidation $Fe^{2+}(aq) \rightarrow Fe^{3+}(aq) + 1e^-$ X 5
Reduction $MnO_4^-(aq) + 5e^- + 8H^+(aq) \rightarrow Mn^{2+}(aq) + 4H_2O(l)$
Net Balanced Redox Reaction:
$5Fe^{2+}(aq) + MnO_4^-(aq) + 8H^+(aq) \rightarrow 5Fe^{3+}(aq) + Mn^{2+}(aq) + 4H_2O(l)$

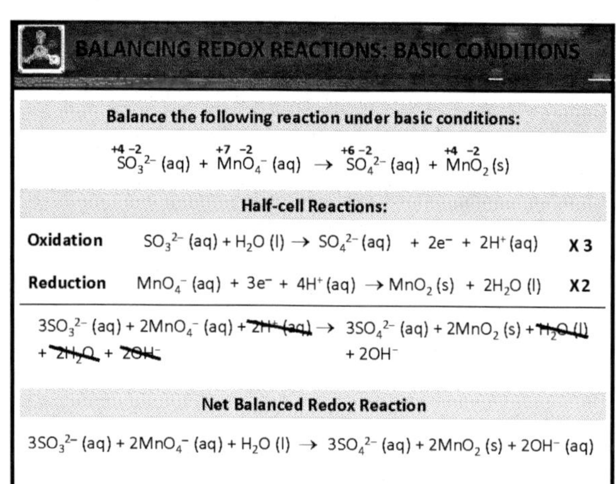

BALANCING REDOX REACTIONS: BASIC CONDITIONS
Balance the following reaction under basic conditions:
$\overset{+4}{S}\overset{-2}{O}{}_3^{2-}(aq) + \overset{+7}{Mn}\overset{-2}{O}{}_4^-(aq) \rightarrow \overset{+6}{S}\overset{-2}{O}{}_4^{2-}(aq) + \overset{+4}{Mn}\overset{-2}{O}{}_2(s)$
Half-cell Reactions:
Oxidation $SO_3^{2-}(aq) + H_2O(l) \rightarrow SO_4^{2-}(aq) + 2e^- + 2H^+(aq)$ X 3
Reduction $MnO_4^-(aq) + 3e^- + 4H^+(aq) \rightarrow MnO_2(s) + 2H_2O(l)$ X2
$3SO_3^{2-}(aq) + 2MnO_4^-(aq) + \cancel{2H^+(aq)} + \cancel{2H_2O} + \cancel{2OH^-} \rightarrow 3SO_4^{2-}(aq) + 2MnO_2(s) + \cancel{H_2O(l)} + 2OH^-$
Net Balanced Redox Reaction
$3SO_3^{2-}(aq) + 2MnO_4^-(aq) + H_2O(l) \rightarrow 3SO_4^{2-}(aq) + 2MnO_2(s) + 2OH^-(aq)$

DISPROPORTIONATION REACTIONS

Decomposition of Hydrogen Peroxide:

H–O–O–H $\quad 2H_2O_2(aq) \rightarrow 2H_2O(l) + O_2(g) \quad \Delta H^\circ < 0$

Half-Reactions:

Oxidation $H_2\overset{-1}{O}_2(aq) \rightarrow \overset{0}{O}_2(g) + 2e^- + 2H^+(aq)$

Reduction $H_2\overset{-1}{O}_2(aq) + 2e^- + 2H^+(aq) \rightarrow 2H_2\overset{-2}{O}(l)$

Overall Equation:

$2H_2O_2(aq) \rightarrow 2H_2O(l) + O_2(g)$

CHECKPOINT

REDOX REACTIONS: EXAMPLES
Silver nitrate
ZINC SULFATE

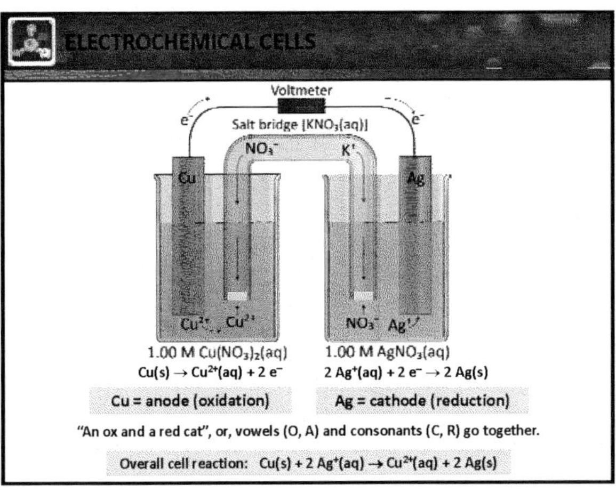
ELECTROCHEMICAL CELLS
Voltmeter
e⁻
Salt bridge [KNO₃(aq)]
NO₃⁻
K⁺
Cu
Ag
Cu²⁺ Cu²⁺
NO₃⁻ Ag⁺
1.00 M Cu(NO₃)₂(aq)
1.00 M AgNO₃(aq)
Cu(s) → Cu²⁺(aq) + 2 e⁻
2 Ag⁺(aq) + 2 e⁻ → 2 Ag(s)
Cu = anode (oxidation)
Ag = cathode (reduction)
"An ox and a red cat", or, vowels (O, A) and consonants (C, R) go together.
Overall cell reaction: Cu(s) + 2 Ag⁺(aq) → Cu²⁺(aq) + 2 Ag(s)

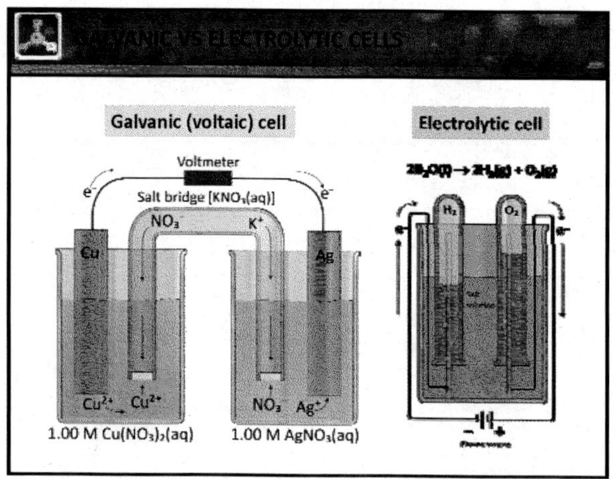
GALVANIC VS ELECTROLYTIC CELLS
Galvanic (voltaic) cell
Electrolytic cell
Voltmeter
Salt bridge [KNO₃(aq)]
Cu
Ag
1.00 M Cu(NO₃)₂(aq)
1.00 M AgNO₃(aq)

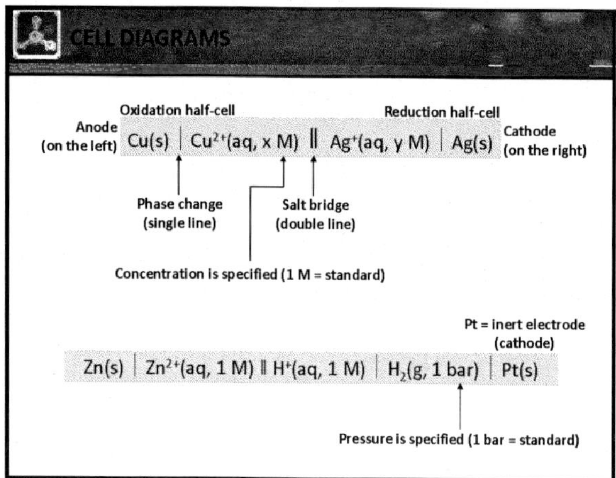
CELL DIAGRAMS
Oxidation half-cell
Reduction half-cell
Anode (on the left)
Cu(s) | Cu²⁺(aq, x M) ‖ Ag⁺(aq, y M) | Ag(s)
Cathode (on the right)
Phase change (single line)
Salt bridge (double line)
Concentration is specified (1 M = standard)
Pt = inert electrode (cathode)
Zn(s) | Zn²⁺(aq, 1 M) ‖ H⁺(aq, 1 M) | H₂(g, 1 bar) | Pt(s)
Pressure is specified (1 bar = standard)

CHECKPOINT

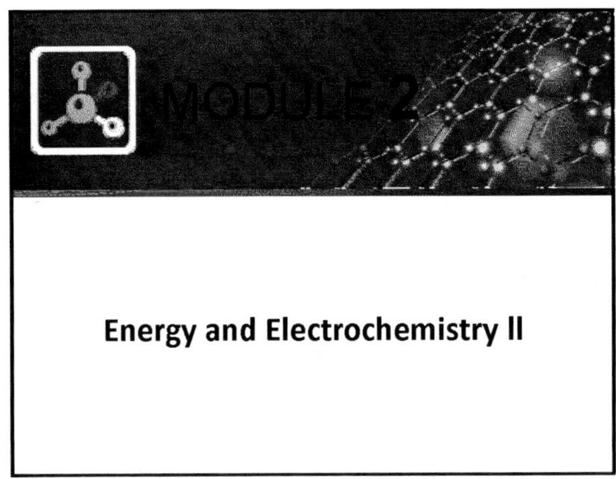
MODULE 2
Energy and Electrochemistry II

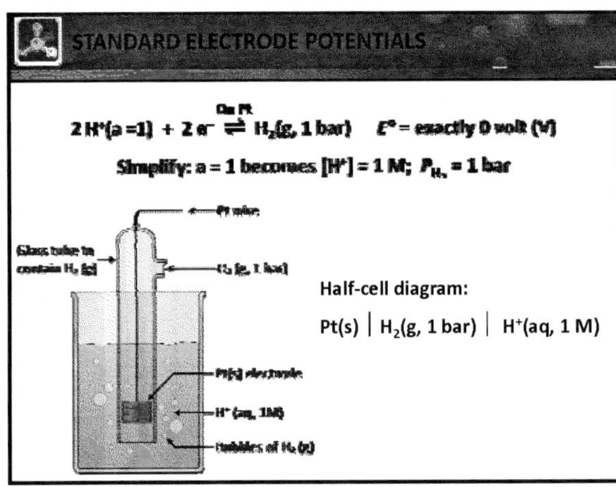
STANDARD ELECTRODE POTENTIALS
$2\,H^+(a=1) + 2\,e^- \underset{}{\overset{\text{On Pt}}{\rightleftharpoons}} H_2(g, 1\ \text{bar})$ $E° =$ exactly 0 volt (V)
Simplify: a = 1 becomes $[H^+] = 1$ M; $P_{H_2} = 1$ bar
Pt wire
Glass tube to contain $H_2(g)$
$H_2(g, 1\ \text{bar})$
Pt(s) electrode
H^+(aq, 1M)
Bubbles of $H_2(g)$
Half-cell diagram:
Pt(s) | H_2(g, 1 bar) | H^+(aq, 1 M)

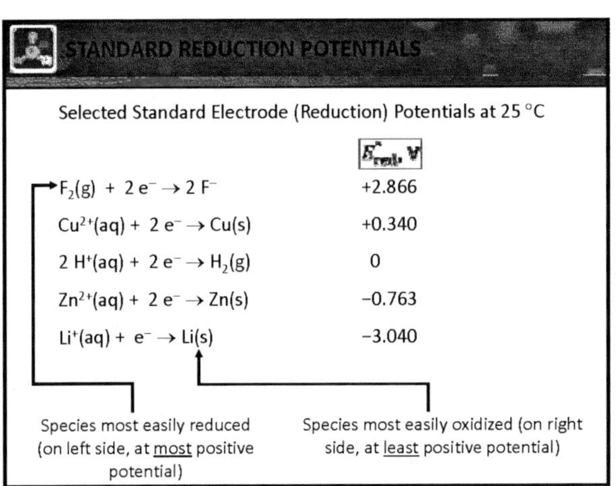
STANDARD REDUCTION POTENTIALS
Selected Standard Electrode (Reduction) Potentials at 25 °C
$E°_{red}$, V
$F_2(g) + 2\,e^- \rightarrow 2\,F^-$ +2.866
$Cu^{2+}(aq) + 2\,e^- \rightarrow Cu(s)$ +0.340
$2\,H^+(aq) + 2\,e^- \rightarrow H_2(g)$ 0
$Zn^{2+}(aq) + 2\,e^- \rightarrow Zn(s)$ −0.763
$Li^+(aq) + e^- \rightarrow Li(s)$ −3.040
Species most easily reduced (on left side, at most positive potential)
Species most easily oxidized (on right side, at least positive potential)

STANDARD CELL POTENTIALS (E^{o}_{cell})

$E^\circ_{cell} = E^\circ(\text{cathode(right)}) - E^\circ(\text{anode(left)})$

$Cu(s)\ |\ Cu^{2+}(aq, 1\ M)\ \|\ Ag^{+}(aq, 1\ M)\ |\ Ag(s)$

ALTERNATIVELY

$E^\circ_{red} = 2Ag^{+}(aq) + 2e^{-} \rightarrow 2Ag(s)$ +0.799 V

$Cu^{2+}(aq) + 2e^{-} \rightarrow Cu(s)$ +0.340 V

$E^\circ_{ox} = Cu(s) \rightarrow Cu^{2+}(aq) + 2e^{-}$ −0.340 V (= $-E^\circ_{red}(Cu)$)

$$\boxed{E^\circ_{cell} = E^\circ_{red} + E^\circ_{ox}}$$

$E^\circ_{cell} = 2Ag^{+}(aq) + Cu \rightarrow 2Ag(s) + Cu^{2+}(aq)$ +0.459 V

STANDARD CELL POTENTIALS (E^{o}_{cell})

1) E° is an intensive property

$2Ag^{+}(aq) + 2e^{-} \rightarrow 2Ag(s)$ $E^\circ_{red} = +0.799$ V

$Ag^{+}(aq) + e^{-} \rightarrow Ag(s)$ $E^\circ_{red} = +0.799$ V

2) $E^\circ_{cell} > 0$ = spontaneous

$Cu^{2+}(aq) + Zn \rightarrow Cu(s) + Zn^{2+}(aq)$ $E^\circ_{cell} = +1.100$ V

$2Ag^{+}(aq) + Cu \rightarrow 2Ag(s) + Cu^{2+}(aq)$ $E^\circ_{cell} = +0.459$ V

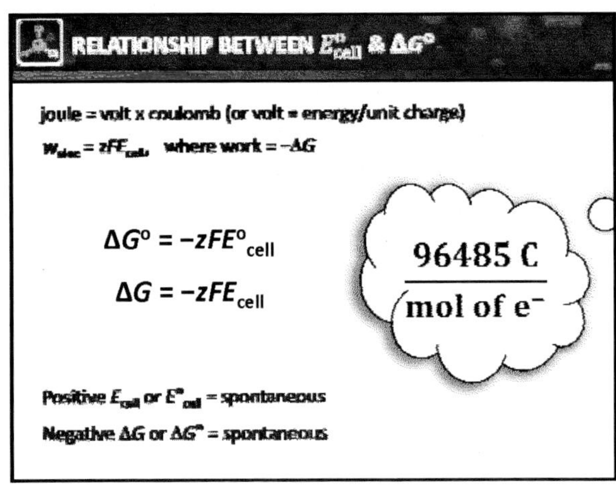
RELATIONSHIP BETWEEN E^{o}_{cell} & ΔG°
joule = volt x coulomb (or volt = energy/unit charge)
$w_{elec} = zFE_{cell}$, where work = $-\Delta G$
$\Delta G^{o} = -zFE^{o}_{cell}$
$\Delta G = -zFE_{cell}$
96485 C / mol of e⁻
Positive E_{cell} or E^{o}_{cell} = spontaneous
Negative ΔG or ΔG^{o} = spontaneous

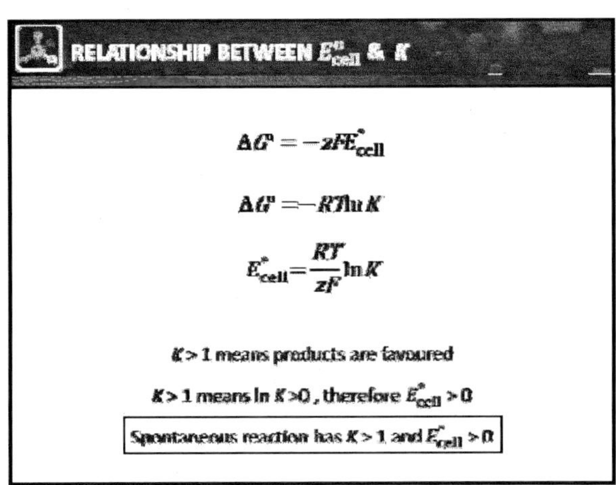
RELATIONSHIP BETWEEN E^{o}_{cell} & K
$\Delta G^{o} = -zFE^{o}_{cell}$
$\Delta G^{o} = -RT\ln K$
$E^{o}_{cell} = \frac{RT}{zF}\ln K$
K > 1 means products are favoured
K > 1 means ln K > 0, therefore $E^{o}_{cell} > 0$
Spontaneous reaction has K > 1 and $E^{o}_{cell} > 0$

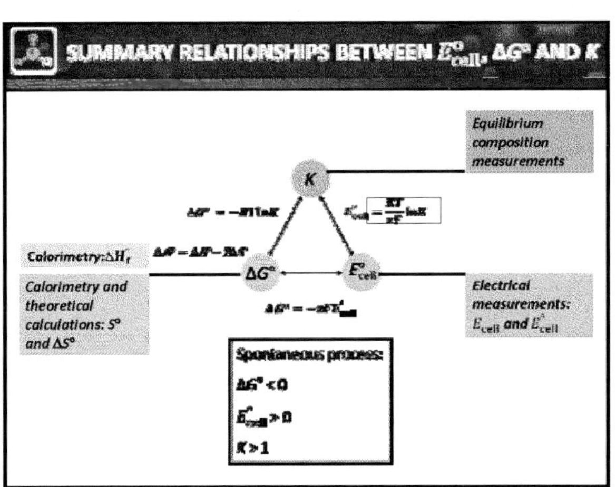
SUMMARY RELATIONSHIPS BETWEEN E^{o}_{cell}, ΔG° AND K
Equilibrium composition measurements
K
$\Delta G^{o} = -RT\ln K$
$E^{o}_{cell} = \frac{RT}{zF}\ln K$
Calorimetry: ΔH_{r}
Calorimetry and theoretical calculations: S° and ΔS°
ΔG°
E^{o}_{cell}
$\Delta G^{o} = -zFE^{o}_{cell}$
Electrical measurements: E_{cell} and E^{o}_{cell}
Spontaneous process:
ΔG° < 0
$E^{o}_{cell} > 0$
K > 1

SAMPLE PROBLEMS

1. Calculate $\Delta G°$ for the spontaneous cell produced from the following:

	$E°_{red}$, V
$Al^{3+}(aq) + 3e^- \rightarrow Al(s)$	−1.676
$Mg^{2+}(aq) + 2e^- \rightarrow Mg(s)$	−2.356

2. Calculate K for the same spontaneous cell, at 25°C.

SOLUTIONS

1.

	$E°_{red}$, V
$Al^{3+}(aq) + 3e^- \rightarrow Al(s)$	−1.676
$Mg^{2+}(aq) + 2e^- \rightarrow Mg(s)$	−2.356
$Mg(s) \rightarrow Mg^{2+}(aq) + 2e^-$	+2.356

Oxidation: $3Mg(s) \rightarrow 3Mg^{2+}(aq) + 6e^-$ $\quad E°_{ox} = +2.356$ V

Reduction: $2Al^{3+}(aq) + 6e^- \rightarrow 2Al(s)$ $\quad E°_{red} = -1.676$ V

Overall: $2Al^{3+}(aq) + 3Mg(s) \rightarrow 2Al(s) + 3Mg^{2+}(aq)$ $\quad E°_{cell} = 0.680$ V and $z = 6$

$\Delta G° = -zFE°_{cell}$

$\Delta G° = -(6 \text{ mol } e^-)(96485 \text{ C/mol } e^-)(0.680 \text{ V})$

$= -393,659$ VC or -393.7 kJ

SOLUTIONS

2. *Calculating K*:

$$\Delta G° = -RT\ln K \quad \text{or} \quad E°_{cell} = \frac{RT}{zF}\ln K$$

$\Delta G° = -RT\ln K$ or $\ln K = -\Delta G°/RT$

$\ln K = -(-393,659 \text{ J}) / [(8.314 \text{ J K}^{-1} \text{ mol}^{-1})(298 \text{ K})]$

$\ln K = 15\underline{8}.889$

$K = e^{158.889} = 1.01 \times 10^{69}$

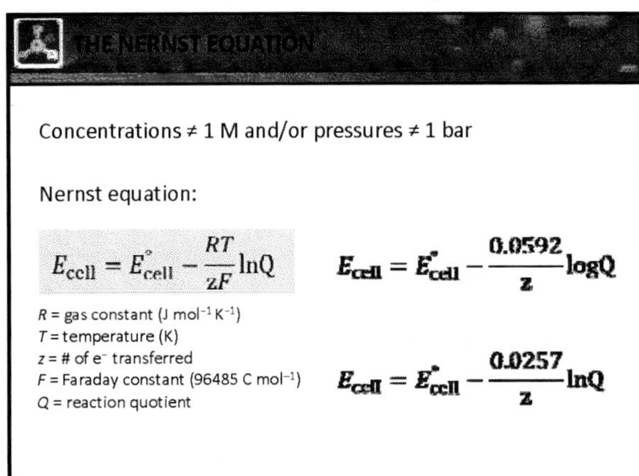
THE NERNST EQUATION
Concentrations ≠ 1 M and/or pressures ≠ 1 bar
Nernst equation:
$E_{cell} = E^{\circ}_{cell} - \frac{RT}{zF}\ln Q$
$E_{cell} = E^{\circ}_{cell} - \frac{0.0592}{z}\log Q$
$E_{cell} = E^{\circ}_{cell} - \frac{0.0257}{z}\ln Q$
R = gas constant (J mol^{-1} K^{-1})
T = temperature (K)
z = # of e$^-$ transferred
F = Faraday constant (96485 C mol^{-1})
Q = reaction quotient

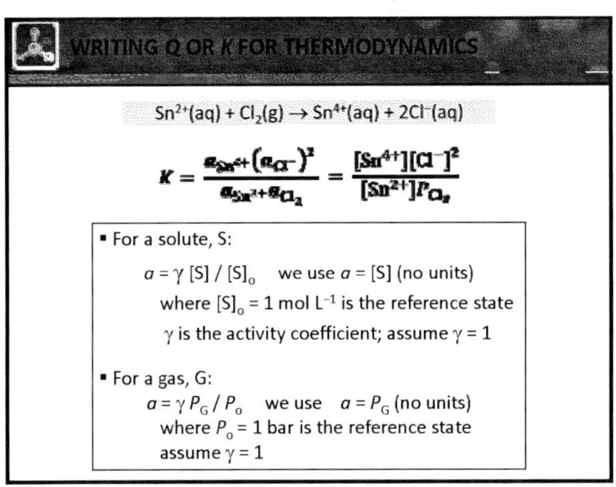
WRITING Q OR K FOR THERMODYNAMICS
$Sn^{2+}(aq) + Cl_2(g) \rightarrow Sn^{4+}(aq) + 2Cl^-(aq)$
$K = \frac{a_{Sn^{4+}}(a_{Cl^-})^2}{a_{Sn^{2+}}a_{Cl_2}} = \frac{[Sn^{4+}][Cl^-]^2}{[Sn^{2+}]P_{Cl_2}}$
▪ For a solute, S:
$a = \gamma\,[S]/[S]_o$ we use a = [S] (no units)
where $[S]_o$ = 1 mol L^{-1} is the reference state
γ is the activity coefficient; assume $\gamma = 1$
▪ For a gas, G:
$a = \gamma P_G / P_o$ we use $a = P_G$ (no units)
where P_o = 1 bar is the reference state
assume $\gamma = 1$

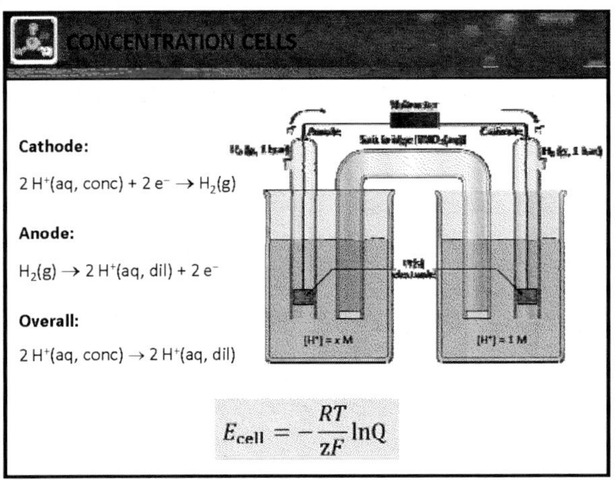
CONCENTRATION CELLS
Cathode:
$2\,H^+(aq, conc) + 2\,e^- \rightarrow H_2(g)$
Anode:
$H_2(g) \rightarrow 2\,H^+(aq, dil) + 2\,e^-$
Overall:
$2\,H^+(aq, conc) \rightarrow 2\,H^+(aq, dil)$
$[H^+] = x$ M
$[H^+] = 1$ M
$E_{cell} = -\frac{RT}{zF}\ln Q$

CHECKPOINT

OBJECTIVES

1. Determine oxidation numbers in reactants and products of redox reactions, and identify oxidizing and reducing agents
2. Balance redox reactions, including those occurring in acidic or basic solution
3. Draw and describe the components and workings of galvanic cells, and write cell diagrams
4. Describe the standard hydrogen electrode and calculate standard cell potentials from standard reduction potentials
5. Use the relationships which link E^{o}_{cell}, ΔG^{o} and K to calculate any of these quantities
6. Use the Nernst equation to determine E_{cell} under non-standard conditions

Unit 10

Most important concepts:

-
-
-
-
-
-
-
-
-
-
-
-

Unit 10

Questions I have:

-
-
-
-
-
-
-
-
-
-
-
-

Intro Chem Course Noteboook

Congratulations!

You have completed viewing all of the Units. Be sure to review all of your notes about "Questions" you had for each Unit, and make sure your questions got answered. As a final reminder of where you can get help:

Resources Available to Help With This Course:

- **Web modules in Avenue to Learn**
- **Course Notebook**
- **Course Textbook (Petrucci, 10th edition)**
- **Help Centre in ABB 307**
- **Instructor and Lab Coordinator Office Hours**
- **Tutorials**
- **Lists of Learning Objectives**
- **In-class Slides**
- **Recommended Practice Questions**
- **Avenue to Learn Discussion Forum**
- **Private Tutor (see list in Avenue to Learn)**

Add in other resources if you have them:

-
-
-